BREAKING FREE

THE KEY TO EMPOWERMENT, HAPPINESS & FULFILLMENT
A CARIBBEAN PERSPECTIVE

DAVID SAMUEL GREEN

Foreword by Dr Kent D. Maxwell

© Copyright 2006 David Samuel Green
10 9 8 7 6 5 4 3 2 1

All rights reserved. No part of this book may be reproduced, stored in a retrieval system, or transmitted, in any form or by any means, electronic, mechanical, photocopying, recording, or otherwise, without the prior written permission of the publishers or author.

If you have bought this book without a cover you should be aware that it is "stolen" property. The publishers/author have not received any payment for the "stripped" book, if it is printed without their authorization.

Executive Editor: Julia Tan
Cover and Book Design: Sanya Dockery

Published by
LMH Publishing Limited
Suite 10, 7 Norman Road
Kingston, C.S.O.
Tel: (876) 938-0005
Fax: (876) 759-8752
Email: lmhbookpublishing@cwjamaica.com

Printed and Bound in USA   ISBN: 976-8202-21-1

This book is dedicated with sincere gratitude and love to Mrs. Hyacinth Brown and Ms Vivia Bryan, two teachers who believed in me and fostered my development, my wife Amoy Nicole Marshall Green, who empowers me daily and my son Jonathan David Samuel Green, who gives me reason to relax and reflect.

CONTENTS

	Page
Foreword	v
Preface	vii
Acknowledgements	ix
Introduction	xi

Part I: Understanding Myself — 1
- Chapter 1   Issues Faced — 2
- Chapter 2   Attitudes Developed — 16
- Chapter 3   Cognitive and Behavioural Consequences of Issues Faced — 24
- Chapter 4   Emotional Consequences of Issues Faced — 48

Part II: Creating a New Self — 57
- Chapter 5   Truths About Self — 59
- Chapter 6   Master Fighter — 70
- Chapter 7   Keen Individual — 76

Part III: Facing the Future with Courage — 93
- Chapter 8   Aspiring for Excellence — 94
- Chapter 9   Coping Strategies — 102
- Chapter 10 Things that Fuel Low Self-Esteem — 109
- Chapter 11 Yielding to God — 126

Reference — 133

FOREWORD

The subject of this book by Mr. David Samuel Green is a timely one for the children of Jamaica. It is a subject with which Mr. Green is very familiar, having served both as a pastor, youth director and as a guidance counsellor in a high school in Jamaica. The issues discussed in the book are issues which he has confronted in these roles, especially his role as a guidance counsellor.

A few years ago, Mr. Green undertook a project to help young men — teenagers in particular — to see themselves realistically and to help them develop a sense of self-esteem and self-worth to enable them to make a contribution to their society regardless of their background respective. He was very successful in this endeavour and enjoyed the recognition of his peers and others because of the difference he was making in the lives of troubled young people. Now, he has put the concepts he discovered and the interventions he developed in addressing this problem into a book to assist others trying to make a difference in the lives of those who work with young persons in Jamaica. Guidance counsellors, teachers, pastors, social workers and others will find this publication invaluable.

It has been my privilege to know Mr. Green for three plus years. As a lecturer and Director of the Counselling Psychology Programme at the Caribbean Graduate School of Theology, he was one of my students, who later served as my teaching assistant. I found him to be a very perceptive young man who takes seriously his responsibility to make a difference in his culture, country, and the lives of those who are struggling with issues they find difficult to handle. Not only is he socially and culturally sensitive, he is also a deeply spiritual individual who understands himself to be a person not of the world but in the world to make a difference for the Christ he serves and the Kingdom of God. He knows the Scriptures and is able to see how they apply in his everyday life and the lives of those he has been called to serve.

It is without reservation, after having read the manuscript twice for the book, that I recommend *Breaking Free: The Key to Empowerment, Happiness and Fulfillment — A Caribbean Perspective* to everyone who wants to make a difference in the lives of children, youth, and eventually adults in the Jamaican society. I am also confident that the concepts and interventions contained in the book are applicable to other societies both within and beyond the Caribbean.

Kent D. Maxwell, D. Min.
January 2006

Given the current social challenges that bombard our youth and other personal and familial issues with which they have to encounter on a daily basis, this book, I believe, has the potential to be a significant asset to the targeted population. The themes are relevant, and its content has many positive inspirational and motivational strategies that young people can employ as they seek to surmount those challenges and become self-fulfilled.

Consequently I endorse the work and effort of Mr. David Samuel Green for compiling this volume to add to the repertoire of literature that is relevant to the Jamaican/Caribbean population that no doubt can be used by parents, teachers, counsellors and other professionals to enhance the quality of life of those young persons with whom they interact.

Grace A. Kelly, PhD
Chairperson
Department of Behavioral Science
Northern Caribbean University

President,
Jamaica Association of Guidance Counsellors in Education

PREFACE

Statistics have shown that many persons in our society have suffered from some form of abuse: physical, emotional, verbal, psychological or mental. As a result of this abuse, they feel worthless, hopeless, helpless, ashamed, dirty, lonely, unloved, unaccepted, guilty and suicidal. They have problems forming and maintaining healthy relationships, performing well academically, and setting and achieving goals in life. This book is intended for such individuals. It provides a practical therapeutic or counselling approach which can help these persons process and eliminate the pain, hurt and suffering caused by abuse, neglect and betrayal, and to live a healthy, happy, meaningful and fulfilling life regardless of their past negative experiences.

Many questions have been raised about private counselling practice in Jamaica, which brought to my attention the state of counselling as a profession in our society. There is a negative connotation associated with counselling. As a result, persons do not readily go for counselling. However, people are hurting but are afraid to share their problems with a counsellor because of confidentiality concerns. In addition, they do not want to be seen going to a counsellor because persons will think that they are crazy or something is wrong with them.

While working as a counsellor with the Better Family Life Project, an initiative of the Private Sector Organization of Jamaica (PSOJ) sponsored by Victoria Mutual Building Society (VMBS), persons related experiencing serious hurt and pain, but when referred for counselling they were not prepared to talk with anyone else about their past hurt and pain. In addition, while supervising M. Sc. Counselling students and B. Sc. Social Work students from the University of the West Indies, it was noticed that there were times when they had to deal with reluctant and resistant clients with whom they had no resources to use to accomplish some therapeutic goals.

After writing two articles, one on **Love Our Boys, Empower Them** and the other **Stop the Abuse**, my colleagues suggested that I continue to develop materials to help counsellors. The matter of writing material for school counsellors was one of discussion when I served as Vice President of the Jamaica Association of Guidance Counsellors in Education, Kingston and St. Andrew Region.

As a result of reflecting on the limitations in the material that the counsellor has at his/her disposal, the negative perception towards counselling in our society, lack of culturally relevant resources to help emerging counsellors and the challenge faced by school counsellors, it appeared fruitful and productive to create a self-help tool that counsellors can use to work with their clients or allow clients to use on their own. It is an attempt to bring help to those who need it in a non-threatening professional manner.

ACKNOWLEDGEMENTS

I have always thought that writing a book was hard. However, I have come to recognize that writing a book is easy but editing a book is a mammoth task. It is based on the difficult nature of editing a book that I am perputually grateful for the labour of love of many persons.

Special thanks for the labour of love of Dr. Kent Maxwell who read the first draft and offered valuable suggestions for the improvement of the book. I am especially grateful for his insight on the issue of persons loving themselves versus persons accepting themselves. I am also extremely blessed that he read the final manuscript and wrote the foreword.

Thanks are also due to Linda Harris and Faith St. Catherine, two of my former supervisees from the M.Sc. Counselling Programme at the University of The West Indies (UWI), whose internship I helped to supervise both as site and clinical supervisor, for reading the initial draft and a subsequent update, and providing valuable feedback for the improvement of the book.

Heartfelt gratitude is due to my wife, Amoy Nicole Marshall Green, for her critical suggestions, especially in helping to shape the title of the book, and her understanding and support when I spent hours in the study or left her in bed many nights when she needed my presence or wanted to converse. To my little son, Jonathan David Samuel Green, for being a good sport while I took care of him in the days and worked on the manuscript.

The insights of the following persons have been very helpful: my friend and colleague, Celia Lindsay, who gave timely feedback on making the language slanted towards the target population and Dr. Patricia Outlaw, who gave an important feedback on the importance of avoiding sexist language.

It has been said that many dreams die because they have been shared with the wrong person(s). Therefore, I am grateful to all those whom I shared the dream with and they encouraged me, especially to Rev. W. George Lewis, from the Constant Spring Road Church of God in Jamaica, for giving me the impetus to work on this project, when he brought to my attention the need that existed and suggested that I consider doing some sessions in the church. In addition, thanks for suggesting way ahead of time that I could do the launch at The Cleve Grant Building, which was motivating. Rev. Dr. Dave Gosse, Head of the Interdisciplinary Studies Department at the Caribbean Graduate School of Theology (CGST), Lecturer at the UWI and Christian Education Director of the Church of God in Jamaica, who suggested a time that I needed to finish the book. To all those who have empowered me to 'break free', too numerous to name, and the clients with whom I have worked, I am very grateful. I am very thankful to Mr. Charles Moore and Kevin Sean Harris. However, special thanks must be extended to Kevin Sean Harris for his hard work in sourcing a perfect image for the front cover of the book. Even when I worked him hard (overtime) to find other images, he was very understanding and patient. You have proven to be a very understanding and patient gentleman in putting up with my numerous calls and doing timely follow-up when we experienced unfortunate delays. Heart felt gratitude is also due to Sanya Dockery for helping me to finally develop the rationale for using the image on the front cover. Thanks Sanya for your hard work in type-setting and making the many adjustments from LMH Publishers, who guided me in getting the book into your hands.

Special thanks to Julia Tan, for sharing her insight and research knowledge of the permanent benefits of classical music on the human soul, especially in the transformation of delinquent children and the raising of the intelligence quotient in children.

Thanks to Dr. Richard Musaazi and Christabell Musaazi, Audrey Brooks and Joy Westcarr who read the typed-set manuscript and provided honest, timely and helpful feedback.

Finally, and most importantly, to God, the One whom I serve and adore for giving me the wisdom and insight to write this book. To God belongs the glory in Christ Jesus *"in whom are hidden all the treasures of wisdom and knowledge"* (Colossians 2:3).

INTRODUCTION

Life presents us with various challenges during the different phases that we go through during the lifecycle, the pilgrimage from the womb to the tomb. One's past experiences sometimes cause the development of an unhealthy understanding of one's self and one's needs. The combined effect is a poor self-understanding. Individuals put limitations on themselves because of the hurt, pain and betrayal that they have experienced. These limitations are further entrenched when they believe the lies that others have told them about themselves and the lies they tell themselves. This has caused many persons to live their lives without having power and control over their own destiny. That is to say, they allow past experiences to shackle them. Therefore, these persons consciously or unconsciously allow their minds to focus on the negatives in a self-destructive manner.

Cognitive Behavioural Psychologists like Aaron Beck and Keith Dobson recognized that how a person thinks affects how he feels and acts. This is consistent with what the Bible teaches. *"For as he thinketh in his heart, so is he:"* (Proverbs 23:7, KJV). Therefore, if a person is going to change his/her feeling and action, he/she has to change the way he/she thinks. In thinking, a person has to learn to reword, rephrase, rethink and reflect. This is similar to what psychologists call cognitive restructuring (Corey 2000, 121).

The foundation to building your shattered self-esteem is belief in your God-given potential. It has to do with an understanding that regardless of your past negative experiences, you are shaped for a purpose, which can be fulfilled by God's grace.

It is imperative for you to understand that as a human being, you have the capacity for reflection and introspection. As a result of this, you do not have to allow the past to hold you captive. You are able to work through the past successfully, take hold of the present and build for the future. Norman Vincent Peale said, "People become really quite remarkable when they start thinking that they can do things. When they believe in themselves they have the first secret of success"(Motivational Quotes 2005 - Internet).

This book is guided by the concept that **time in, and of itself, does not heal**. That is, healing does not take place by osmosis. It is what you do with time to facilitate the healing process that makes the difference. All human beings have issues. However, some individuals have taken the time to work through their issues. Therefore, the challenge is for you to take the time to work through your issues, as some of the principles that have been used by others are shared with you. Like Art Williams, I challenge you, "I'm not telling you it is going to be easy - I'm telling you it's going to be worth it" (Motivational Quotes 2005 - Internet). From the outset, you need to tell yourself that life is too precious to be wasted.

The book is divided into three parts. PART I deals with understanding myself, PART II with creating a new self and PART III with facing the future with courage. The book also contains reflections: Part I is geared at helping individuals reflect on their current self-understanding and release themselves from the shackles of the past. The reflections in Part II are geared at helping individuals develop a new self-understanding; and in Part III the reflections are geared at helping individuals embrace the future with courage. "One reason most books don't transform us is that we are so eager to read the next chapter, we don't pause and take the time to seriously consider what we have just read. We rush to the next truth without reflecting on what we have learned" (Warren 2002, 10). Therefore, the reflections are also geared at helping you to avoid this common pitfall in reading books. Take the time to interact with the material. The book can be used in therapy or counselling or by an individual. The reflections can also be used in personal development and career planning courses. It is hoped that this book will help individuals begin the process of maximizing their potential and fulfilling their purpose(s).

PART I

PART I
Understanding Myself

A farmer found a bird in his field one day. He took it home and put it with his chickens. He fed the bird like the chickens. After a while, the farmer was convinced that this bird was also a chicken. The bird behaved like the chickens. The bird lost its identity because it was taken from its family and put in a strange environment and naturally adapted to the norms of the new setting.

This bird continued to be treated like a chicken although it was an eagle. It operated based on what it was accustomed to. It would not fly. It did not know it had the capacity to take on the challenge. It did not know that it could free itself. The eagle was lost in the issues that it faced as it grew. It was cut off from the support and guidance that it needed to learn to fly. The eagle continued to live based on how the past had shaped it. The rest of this story will form the basis for the commencement of Part II.

Like the eagle, some individuals have been shaped negatively by their past experiences. The issues that they faced have caused them to lose sight of their capacity to take control over their lives and free themselves from the shackles of the past. They have become slaves of the past because of their negative experiences without being consciously aware of it.

In this section, the focus is placed on individuals understanding themselves. In CHAPTER 1, the focus will be placed on issues faced by individuals. CHAPTER 2 focuses on negative attitudes that develop as a result of issues faced. In CHAPTER 3, the focus is placed on the cognitive and behavioural consequences of issues faced. In CHAPTER 4, the focus will be on the emotional consequences of issues faced. The reflections, at the end of each chapter is geared at helping individuals to process the hurt, pain and betrayal that they have experienced.

CHAPTER 1
Issues Faced

In this section, the focus is placed on individuals' understanding themselves based on the issues that they faced. There will be an examination of the impact of family, community and society on the person's life. The negative effects of poor parenting and lack of paternal involvement in a child's life will also be given serious attention. The issue of sexual hurt and pain from the perspective of women and men will be analysed. There will be a discussion on the impact of poor role models and the pervasiveness of issues; it is to be understood that everyone has issues. The Reflections at the end of the chapter are geared at helping individuals tell themselves the truth about how they feel based on their past hurt, pain and betrayal.

The pervasiveness of child neglect and abuse varies from society to society and community to community, given the laws and social support that exist in various contexts. This is in sync with a basic premise in sociology, which states that "people's actions are largely influenced by the groups to which they belong and by the interactions that take place within those groups" (Chalfant and LaBeff 1988, 1). However, regardless of the laws and social support, history and statistics have revealed that many persons suffered growing up as children because the law in some instances has not served the purpose of protecting children.

Sociologists argue that the functions of the family encompass sexual regulation, reproduction, socialization, affection, status conferring, protection and economic support (Horton 1965). Sociologists fall short in not including spiritual training as a distinct function of the family. **The function of the family cannot be separated from the spiritual dimension of an individual's life**. This concept has been given credence by the sociologists' recognition that "no family can fully succeed in socializing children in a way of life not practiced by the family" (Horton 1965, 211). That is, if families do not take the spiritual dimension of life seriously, they cannot socialize their children in this vital dimension of life.

Child neglect manifests itself in the style of parenting exercised by the child's parents. Balswick and Balswick (1999) argued that the neglecting parenting style is low in both support and control. That is to say, these parents do not support and offer the necessary boundaries for their children. Consequently child neglect and abuse occur in several ways. Some of these are:

- Failure to warn the child of potential risks and striving to protect the child.
- Not sending the child to school and not being involved in the child's educational development.
- Poor nutrition and medical care.
- Not taking the child's concerns seriously, for example, not believing the child when he or she reports sexual abuse. It has been recognized that "tragedy after tragedy occurs in situations where there is little or no communication between parent and children or where children are not believed" (Prendergast 1996, 59).
- Expecting the child to perform well in school without providing the tools.
- Not developing in the child a sense of right and wrong.
- Leaving the child unsupervised.
- Buying into the culture of communities and putting the child at risk.
- Failure to report offences against children because of concern over one's own life.
- Having more children than one is able to adequately provide for.
- Physically or sexually abusing the child.

The question that arises as a result of the foregoing is: can someone be held responsible for not doing something that he/she did not know that he/she should be doing? As the law says, ignorance is no excuse. There is a principle known as personal responsibility. Therefore, not preparing one's self for the role of parenting can be the premise for child neglect and abuse.

Some children were battered and bruised without "justifiable reasons" (not that abuse can be justified). They bawled without any bosom to breathe on. They writhed in agony and sadness as their problems became painful. Their experience was like a strong tooth being removed without novocaine. For some persons it was not *My Mother Who Fathered Me* (Clarke 1999) but my mother who mobbed me. It was not my parents who cared for me but my parents who scared me.

Some individuals reflect trepidation or fear. Their eyes fill with tears as they remember the tones of venomous proclamations that were pronounced over their lives. It becomes even more painful as they remember how they searched for love and attention and ended up being further abused. According to Cynthia L. Mather (1994, 15), "Much sexual abuse happens under the disguise of love and attention." It gets even more complicated as they reflect on the opinions of sociologists that "victims of abuse…often have very low opinions of themselves. They tend to feel guilty because they question what they have done to deserve such treatment. They sometimes suffer from depression and may have difficulty in close emotional relationships" (Chalfant 1988, 70). The foregoing asserts that **sexual abuse has a serious impact on people's lives**.

The issue of child sexual abuse is so critical it must be given special attention. This special attention is necessary in light of the fact that it is pervasive and has devastating effects. Cynthia L. Mather (1994, 4) asserts, "literally thousands of kids…are trying [or have tried] to protect themselves from the very people who are supposed to love them and take care of them. These kids are being sexually abused by people in their lives whom they have a right to trust and believe will not hurt them." This betrayal is not only traumatic, its negative effects often last a lifetime.

Sexual abuse can be placed in three categories, based on the person who is carrying out the abuse, namely family (incest), someone with care or custody of the child and someone whom the child has no relationship to (sexual assault). Sexual abuse can be defined as someone "taking advantage of a child through any act that is designed to sexually stimulate a child or to use a child to sexually stimulate someone else" (Mather 1994, 5). This definition asserts that a child can be sexually abused actively or passively. Prendergast's (1996, 37) assertion that a child can be traumatized actively or passively gives credence to the aforementioned. The abuse can manifest itself in both sexual contact and non-sexual contact with the child.

Incest is a form of sexual abuse that is both harder to come to terms with and harder to recover from. Incest can be defined as the "sexual abuse of a child by a person who is a member of the child's family or has some type of kinship role in the child's life" (Mather 1994, 6). This is an occurrence that persons are fearful to report or to talk about because of its negative impact on the family. However, the paradox is that **with incest, the family is already being negatively affected**. It is extremely draining and confusing when someone has to be protecting himself/ herself from the person(s) whom he/she should be trusting to care for him/her.

Statistics show that many children have suffered from child neglect and abuse in Jamaica. There are many ways in which children have been neglected by their parents. Some children have suffered from lack of emotional, psychological, material, economic, physical and educational support. They have also suffered from lack of parental involvement from one or both parents. In light of this, childhood neglect can be defined as the failure of a child's parent(s) to adequately provide for him/her and by so doing not fulfilling the roles and functions of the family, such as the basic necessities for food, clothing, shelter, protection, caring attention and emotional support. It is important that these needs are met because "children are malleable…what happens in the early years is important" (Gilbert 1998, 155).

Childhood neglect exposes a child to many serious dangers. Neglected children become more susceptible to sexual abuse and negative peer pressure. Some of these children have searched for love and ended up being taken advantage of. These experiences have caused many persons to feel worthless and ashamed. Willard F. Harley (1997, 157) affirms this by his claim that "low self-esteem, one of the most common problems I help clients overcome, begins very early — in the home, during childhood."

Some individuals have suffered from the ripping effects of being sexually abused. This experience could result from either incest or molestation and sexual assault or rape, which are difficult to live with. As a result, their lives have become a total nightmare and they feel like dying. According to Cynthia L. Mather (1994), the impact of sexual abuse is long lasting in its effects even when the abuse has stopped, unless a person takes the time to process his/her life and make the necessary repairs and adjustments. The good thing, however, as the above asserts, there is hope. A person can take authority over his/her life by working through his/her issues.

The parents of some children have physically abused them. It is difficult when one has to be protecting himself/herself from the person(s) who should be protecting and caring for him/her. It is hard to come to terms with a parent heartless to the point of rubbing pepper in her daughter's vagina. How about using a hot iron and other deadly objects to discipline the child in the name of love and care? What about breaking a child's finger while beating him/her with a mop stick and not taking him/her to get medical attention, causing the child's finger to set in a twisted manner?

It is hard to understand how a parent could give his/her child as a sex mate to someone in return for favours. Indeed, some parents have been the worse nightmares for their children. Also, how could a parent expect a child to perform well in school without the tools to work with?

It is difficult to understand how a parent could constantly tell a child that he/she is 'worthless and good for nothing.' What about 'all you have on your head is man, you can go to your man, do not let me stop you?' What about 'you are a demon?' It is hard to survive through venomous proclamations like these. Physically, such children have "parent(s)". They are there physically providing the basic, or bare essentials of living. Emotionally, such children are orphans, cut off from all emotional support. These parents were at times their child's worst parasites. Their hold on their child's life was like teething and gripping pains that the child was powerless to deal with. At times it was like a dripping pipe in a time of extreme tiredness. Thus, the child felt like disappearing and not be alive at all. Many had to suffer from the heartless, ruthless, rotten and emotionless encounters with their parents and other relatives. Sometimes parent was so engrossed in the evils of the other parent, the child felt totally abandoned and utterly alone.

Other than the parent, whose impact on the child is lifelong, one other person in the child's life has a lifetime influence. This is the teacher. The negative or positive impact of a teacher has a lasting impact. Some teachers have damaged the self-esteem of students severely. When a teacher calls a student or an entire class 'loggerheaded', it is very painful. It is difficult to cope when the persons whom you are expecting to believe in you, and help you, are the very persons who are crushing your self-esteem.

The existing school system has done injustice to a lot of persons. There is "classism" as it relates to which school you went to or are attending.

This is so deeply entrenched that according to Devon Dick (2002, 42), "students define their self-worth and values in terms of the high school attended…," with the traditional high schools in Jamaica being the ideal. This tendency is further complicated when students are streamed in upgraded high schools and treated poorly by teachers.

There are persons who had done well academically but have not gone to traditional high school who feel badly about themselves. That is, even after they have gone to university or college and have done better than those who went to traditional high school, they still feel inferior. However, the irony is that they should feel good about themselves based on the odds that they had to work against to achieve. This problem persists because attending traditional high school "facilitates access to other social groups and linkages to economic opportunity…" (Dick 2002, 42).

When the Alumni Associations of traditional high schools are compared to that of upgraded high schools, it is clear that the self-esteem of persons who went to traditional high school seems to reflect an attitude of being proud of their alma mater based on the membership. Therefore, even the schools which persons went to become an issue that they have to deal with in the job market and in peer groups. **The issue of being at a disadvantage because of the school that they went to has kept some persons at a disadvantage**.

Look at how poorly The Most Hon. Portia Simpson-Miller, Prime Minister of Jamaica, was treated by some persons in the presidential race to succeed The Most Hon. P. J. Patterson as Leader of the People's National Party (PNP) and Prime Minister. She received very harsh criticisms although her experience (nearly forty years in politics) and popularity indicated that she was the favourite candidate. This had a lot to do with her background and education. It is worth noting that she is now ranked at number 89 of the world's 100 most powerful women. She is also the first woman from the English-speaking Caribbean to make the annual list.

It is difficult for children to go through such negative experiences and become well-adjusted individuals. Those who are going through these experiences find it difficult to cope. These kinds of issues have serious impact on a child's ability to learn and be educated and on his/her life as an adult. This is supported by the affirmation of the authors of *Marriage and Family, Annual Edition, 98/99* that "when children have to defend themselves constantly from inside and outside dangers, there is little energy for schoolwork. There is also evidence that specific cognitive functions such as memory and a sense of time can be affected" (Gilbert 1998, 153).

> *Here is a case for examination. There was a bright young lady in Grade 8 in all age school. She grew up with her mother, step-father, four half brothers and one step-brother, while her brother and sister grew up with their father. She was repeatedly abused physically and sexually by her step-father. Her step-father got her pregnant. He told her to go and have sex with a man in the community so she could lay the responsibility on him. She refused to do so. She had the child and had to give the child a strange surname to hide it from her mother and persons in the community. She was literally afraid of her step-father. She was later pushed out of the house by her step-father, leaving her daughter with her mother and step-father.*

In the above case, it is prudent to say that Solomon is right in his claim that, "*A man's spirit sustains him in sickness, but a crushed spirit who can bear?*" (Proverbs. 18:14). Solomon is right because sickness will be healed with time but when the spirit is broken by psychological and emotional pain, it can continue to have a negative impact on a person for the rest of his/her life. Gary Chapman (2004, 181) affirms this in his conclusion that "hundreds of thirty-five-year-old adults still hear words of condemnation spoken twenty years ago ringing in their ears…"

Challenges Faced by Young Men

In our Jamaican society, when males are sexually abused it is not treated with the kind of negative reactions as when females are sexually abused. However, while growing up, some boys have been sexually abused by older women. This has serious impact on a boy's life and he is not encouraged to talk about the hurt and pain that he is experiencing. He would be frowned at as being soft or "funny" if he talks negatively about those frightening experiences.

If he talks about passes made on him by homosexual(s) or bisexual(s), he would be looked-down on as the one with whom something is wrong. He does not get proper information about these issues and their effects, so he goes around hurting and engaging in sexual activities without even knowing what is driving him. In short, his own behaviour is not even understood by him.

It is a great possibility that sexual initiation of boys by older women has a negative effect on the male attitude towards sex and women. A boy who was sexually abused grows up thinking that women need him and he has to help them out. This also probably has a bearing on the issue of lack of self-control and self-discipline as it relates to sexual activities.

> ***Take this case for example.*** *A boy was initiated into sexual activity by his 12-year-old female cousin when he was seven-years-old and his parents knew about it and did nothing. At age eight he was taken to spend the holiday with his mother's friend and was sexually abused most nights by the two daughters of his mother's friend (8-years-old and 14-years-old) for one summer. He never used to wet his bed but started wetting bed because of the abuse. He was abused sexually by his 15-year-old sister when he was ten years old. He was sexually abused by his next-door neighbour's 16-year-old daughter when he was eleven years old. From the ages of 7-12 years, his cousin, mentioned above, continued to abuse him sexually (even while she was seeing her period). His 12-year-old male cousin, brother of his female cousin, tried to have anal sex with him when he was about nine years old. He told his parents about it and they did nothing. When he was 18, he was approached by a bisexual male.*

The above mentioned case is a good example of the kinds of issues with which males have to deal. These kinds of issues cause deep hurt and pain that are not spoken about. This is not an issue for males only from the so called "ghetto". **Males do hurt and are not given the kind of attention that they need to face and deal with issues like these.**

Poor Role Models

It has been vehemently argued that it takes more than just an immediate family to raise a child; it takes a community. In light of this reality, poor role models both in the home and society have affected the lives of many persons negatively. The moral laxity in society has created cognitive dissonance, which has to do with being frustrated and confused because of what one is told to do and what one observes being done, even by those who gave the instruction.

The social psychologists talk about observational learning, which helps to elucidate the concept of role models. Albert Bandura as referenced by Tuner and Helms (1995), explored the concept of observational learning (which has to do with what one learns by watching other people's behaviours) and championed the dynamics of the social learning theory. **Poor role models cause some individuals to hold on to the wrong values**. It also causes them to want to be like the wrong individuals, which results in some individuals constantly trying to be whom they were not meant to be.

In the Jamaican society, coming out of the experience of slavery, as studied by Edith Clarke (1999), there seemed to have been a sexual practice among males and females which fostered the irresponsibility of males in not taking care of their children. Regrettably, this phenomenon still persists today contributing to the many prevalent problems of Jamaica. According to Devon Dick (2002, 54), "majority of children do not have their fathers' names on their birth certificates." The nature of the example that is being set for this generation is woefully catastrophic. It sets the stage for total disaster on a massive scale for the nation. This situation has been further complicated by the pragmatic orientation (making condoms available and accessible to persons under the age of sixteen) that is being advocated in an attempt to deal with the social challenges (like HIV/AIDS or sexual activity among minors in the Jamaican society). This approach is diametrically opposed to the law of the land which purports that a person should not engage in sexual activity with anyone below the age of sixteen (16).

The role models of many individuals are morally and ethically bankrupt. However, it is not easily recognized that the role models are causing them to travel on a collision course with disaster. The problem lies in the fact that the "in thing" has a way of becoming the "right thing" when it is not so. This no doubt causes serious physical, emotional and psychological consequences. The society and community at large, have given too much audience to the wrong role models, resulting in some individuals adopting their behaviours. It is important to remember that "People are first influenced by what they see…modelling can be a powerful influence- either positively or negatively" (Maxwell and Dornan 1997, 6).

Pervasiveness of Issues

Issues are no respecter of person. Therefore, issues are not gender biased although the nature of some issues is gender specific. In light of this, some individuals have rightly argued that "we all have issues". An author has even developed the concept. *"The Wounded Healer"* (Henri Nouwen 1979), suggests that counsellors must go through their issues so they can help others through the process. From a Biblical perspective, the concept is accurate because of the sinful nature of the world.

At times individuals believe that they are the only ones who are faced with certain issues. This is not so. It only appears this way because most people do not like to talk about their negative experiences. They psychologically block out the hurt and pain they experienced. It is, therefore, important to understand that individuals are hurting for various reasons. It is important to note that, "many lives are scarred and personalities warped because of unjust treatment received as children" (Snyder 1985, 56). No one can say to others, 'you should not be hurting over that,' because each individual reacts differently to situations. The important thing is for individuals to be committed to working through their issues. But to work through issues the individual first and foremost, has to acknowledge that issues do exist.

A part of the hope of an individual successfully working through his/her issues lies in the fact that **brokenness is common to human experience**. This 'brokeness' has a Biblical perspective; what is broken can be made whole again, albeit by God's help. **Vessels of honour can be created out of broken vessels, no matter how broken they have been**. In addition, others have taken control over their lives by working through their issues. Each individual has the potential and capacity to do the same and take control over his/her life and destiny.

Reflections

Telling Myself the Truth

1. Recall and write down the most emotionally painful experiences that you have had.

   ....
   ....
   ....
   ....
   ....
   ....
   ....
   ....
   ....

2. Reflect on the experiences and write down your reaction to the following:
   (a) Your thoughts about yourself

   ....
   ....
   ....
   ....

(b) Your thoughts about other people

....
....
....
....

(c) Your thoughts about the future

....
....
....
....
....
....

(d) Your thoughts about God

....
....
....
....
....
....
....
....

(e) Your thoughts about family

....
....
....
....
....
....

3. Review your emotionally painful experiences and write down your reaction to the following:

   (a) I am responsible for my emotionally painful experiences.

   ....
   ....
   ....
   ....
   ....
   ....

   (b) My parents are responsible for my emotionally painful experiences.

   ....
   ....
   ....
   ....
   ....
   ....
   ....
   ....
   ....

   (c) Other persons are responsible for my emotionally painful experiences.

   ....
   ....
   ....
   ....
   ....
   ....

(d) There is shared responsibility for my emotionally painful experiences.

....
....
....
....
....
....

CHAPTER 2
Attitudes Developed

In this section, the focus is placed on individuals understanding themselves based on the attitudes that they developed as a result of the issues that they faced. The discussion recognizes that one's attitude determines how he/she deals with the past to take hold of the future. It also develops the concept of four categories of persons based on how they deal with their past hurt, pain and betrayal. The Reflections help individuals to ponder on and process their past hurt, pain and betrayal and place responsibility where it belongs.

The hurt and pain that individuals have experienced from the issues that they faced have a direct impact on their attitudes towards life, people, relationships, goals, parents or God. The hurt and pain that individuals have experienced may contribute to their developing an attitude of getting even (revenge), passivity (whatever happens, happens), offering cheap forgiveness or assuming inappropriate responsibility.

The attitude of striving to get even (revenge) causes individuals to do things purposely to hurt others. It is not about getting justice but about repaying evil for evil. This attitude of getting even does not solve the problem because the cycle continues for a life time without any justice, creating greater problem for the individuals. It is a self-destructive approach in dealing with hurt, pain and betrayal. It continues endlessly, doing just the opposite. It actually intensifies the hurt, pain and betrayal.

In developing a passive attitude, individuals tell themselves that their goals are not important. They are not worthwhile, whatever happens, happens. They blindly tell themselves that they do not care. The irony, however, is that they spend time complaining about what they do not have. This suggests that deep down they really care. It is self-destructive to develop this kind of attitude because it causes individuals to give others power to control their lives and destiny. They begin to see others as important and themselves as serving no purpose.

This makes individuals put their lives on an eternal hold. As a result, they do not set goals for their lives and work at accomplishing them. The root of this has to do with the fact that these individuals no longer believe in themselves. They have allowed past negative experiences to cloud their innate capacity for success.

Individuals sometimes engage in offering cheap forgiveness. That is, they forgive those who have hurt them without processing the hurt and pain that others have caused them. They do not allow themselves to experience the hurt and pain that others have caused. They justify the actions of others towards them. They forgive too easily and put themselves at risk which results in further hurt and they continue the deadly cycle allowing their lives to continue on a collision course with disaster.

Individuals sometimes take inappropriate responsibility for the hurt, pain and betrayal that they experienced. They hold themselves responsible for what they had no control over. This attitude causes them to see themselves as the evil ones when, in fact, they are the victims. They therefore engage in taking responsibility for people's actions when they are responsible only for their own actions. In short, they are preyed upon by people who manipulate them.

These four attitudes are deadly for four main reasons:
1   Individuals do not allow themselves to feel the hurt, pain and betrayal that they experienced.
2   Individuals do not hold others appropriately responsible for the hurt, pain and betrayal that they have caused.
3   These kinds of attitudes do not allow individuals to successfully get over their past.
4   These attitudes do not give individuals the ammunition that they need to deal successfully with life's challenges.

This therefore, suggests that individuals live their lives based on an external locus of control. That is, they have given others power to control them. Therefore, either they continue to have the wrong attitude and allow their lives to continue to operate on an external locus of control or change their attitude and develop an internal locus of control. They should either take control over their lives by changing their attitude or continue to give others that control. This requires getting rid of what Mulholland (1993, 127) calls "those old harmful habits, those deeply ingrained imprisoning attitudes, those troubling and damaging perspectives, those destructive ways of relating to others, those unhealthy modes of reacting and responding to the world…"

Abuse, betrayal and neglect create four types of persons. These types can be labelled the refuters, receivers, rejecters and reflectors. The refuters are those who deny that the abuse, betrayal or neglect ever took place or is taking place. They refuse to see the persons who are hurting or have hurt them in a negative light. They deny that the abuse is taking place or has taken place to numb the pain. They blot the memories connected with the hurt. However, like William Glasser's Reality Therapy, referenced by Jones and Butman (1991) indicates, these persons need to recognize that if it is happening, it is happening; or if it had happened, it had happened. When one denies that the abuse or neglect took place, it causes the abuse or neglect to wreak havoc on one's life. **The refuters can consciously suppresss painful memories but such memories live on in the subconscious mind**. So they are fighting a losing battle. And their own lives will continue to get worse.

The receivers are those who passively accept the abuse or neglect. They hold themselves totally responsible for what took place or is taking place. However, the reality is, they are never the cause of abuse or neglect. Nichols and Schwartz (2004, 86) support this by affirming that, "abused children need to hear over and over that what happened was not their fault." **Accepting inappropriate responsibility causes these persons to engage in unhealthy behaviours, at times, in risqué sexual conduct**. According to Gary Chapman (2004, 179), "If all goes well and their emotional needs are met, children develop into responsible adults; but if the emotional need is not met, they may violate acceptable standards…seeking love in inappropriate places." This leads to further hurt and pain complicating their lives and its healing process.

The rejecters are those who refuse to take responsibility for the abuse or the neglect. They have chosen to adjust their lives in a manner that allows them to place blame where it must be placed. **They are willing**

to face the issue head-on in order to recover. They refuse to remain in the victim role and strive instead to become victors.

The reflectors are those who are willing to do the work necessary to recover from the devastating effects of abuse, betrayal or neglect. They are willing to process the issue and allow themselves to feel the hurt and pain that the abuse, betrayal or neglect caused. **They are able to allow themselves to feel the range of emotions caused by the abuse, betrayal or neglect.** They are willing to get past their past without passing over their past. That is, they are willing to work through their hurt, pain and betrayal in order to maximize their potential. It should be noted that some persons vacillate between being the refuter, receiver, rejecter and reflector on the road to recovery.

> *Here is a case for reflection on one's attitude.* A gentleman had a water problem where he and his family lived. Therefore, an air-tank was put in place to deal with the problem whenever water goes from the main. He had to turn off the main pipe to prevent the water from running out of the tank to the main. One evening the pressure in the tank went low so he went and turned on the main to see if the water was back. He then went and checked but there was no water.
>
> There was no water in the house for three days. He had to try to catch water whenever it rained and his wife took some containers to her workplace and brought home water. He went out one day and came in very thirsty and had no water to drink.
>
> On the fourth morning his wife said to him, 'Honey, are you sure you turned on that pipe?' He responded 'Yes, I did.' Thinking to himself, 'Does she think that I am crazy, would I be here without water for so many days and not know whether or not the pipe is on?' He was reluctant to get up out of bed and check. He decided to check the pipe later in the day and recognized that he did not turn it on. There was water in the main.

The case quoted is a very good illustration of what will happen to a person without the right attitude. If the gentleman did not have the right attitude he would have continued without water, when water was available. If a person does not have the right attitude he/she will not be able to break free from the shackles, and he/she will continue to suffer unnecessarily. This is so, despite the fact that actual help or 'tools' are offered. The gentleman did something to get water; **you have to be**

prepared to do something to get what you need. W. Clement Stone said, "There is little difference in people, but that little difference makes a big difference. The little difference is attitude. The big difference is whether it is positive or negative" (Motivational Quotes 2005 - Internet). You need to make and value small changes because this is important in breaking "inertia and initiate movement in a positive direction" (Benner 2003, 44).

Reflections

Processing Feelings

1. Review your notes on your emotionally painful experiences and write down your current reflection.

   ....
   ....
   ....
   ....
   ....
   ....
   ....

2. Rebuke those who have hurt you emotionally by:
   (a) Allowing yourself to feel all the hurt and pain that you have experienced. I am feeling:

   ....
   ....
   ....
   ....
   ....

(b) Give them total responsibility for their actions. You are responsible for:

....
....
....
....
....
....
....

(c) Allow yourself to feel appropriate anger for the person(s) who have hurt you. I am angry with you because:

....
....
....
....
....
....
....
....
....
....
....

(d) Place responsibility for your hurt and pain appropriately where it belongs. I give responsibility for my hurt and pain to the following:

....
....
....
....
....
....
....

3. What hurt, pain and betrayal have you experienced?

   ....
   ....
   ....
   ....
   ....
   ....

4. Four categories of persons were discussed (refuter, receiver, rejecter, and reflector). Which one are you? Provide reasons for your answer.

   ....
   ....
   ....
   ....
   ....
   ....
   ....
   ....
   ....
   ....
   ....

CHAPTER 3

Cognitive and Behavioural Consequences of Issues Faced

In this section, the focus is placed on individuals understanding the cognitive and behavioural consequences that they are experiencing, based on the issues that they faced. The discussion reveals that one's thoughts and beliefs are very powerful and are also very important components of one's health and well-being. The concept and analogy of the cancerous mind, heart, feet, hand, eye, and ears is explored to paint a vivid picture of how the past causes persons to think, feel and act. The Reflections aim at helping individuals to confront their negative thoughts and beliefs that are working against them.

The Cancerous Mind

In every area of life, there are principles of engagement. That is, there are principles that guide one's thoughts, actions, reactions and responses. Some of these principles of engagement are noticeable while others are unnoticeable. There is a serious problem when one's principles of engagement are built on lies.

It is difficult for some persons to admit that, sometimes, they are their own parasites. This is so because their cognitive processes, which are built on lies, cause their minds to operate like cancerous cells. They damage themselves based on their internal dialogue, be it consciously or unconsciously. That is, they give birth to "cancerous cells" that sustain them through destructive patterns of thinking and acting. Sometimes the cancerous cell is not easily seen, which makes it difficult for them to be aware of its progressive effects. M. Scott Peck (1983, 62) emphasises that "when we are adults the greater part of our thought life proceeds on the unconscious level. For children and young adolescents, almost all mental activity is unconscious."

The cancerous mind is very dangerous and hard to deal with because it influences every area of a person's life. These individuals tell themselves that they are victims of circumstances and are unable to survive the devastating effects of the traumas and crises that they experienced. Thus, they volunteer to remain captives of their circumstances. The paradox is that they become their own victims, destroying themselves and laying the blame solely on others for their condition when they are the ones who have refused to take action to better their lives.

The cancerous mind, therefore, provides the base for lies to dominate their lives. They tell themselves that they are worthless, good-for-nothing and unable to get past their past without passing over their past. That is, they are unable to successfully deal with their past failures, abuses and broken relationships. They tell themselves that they are totally responsible for the things that happened to them.

Sometimes it is very difficult for persons to deal with compliments because they are not accustomed to being complimented. When someone gives a genuine compliment, it is interpreted negatively based on the negative evaluation that characterizes the person's life. The thought process of the person is negative, which causes him/her to accuse the one giving the compliment of not being real or genuine. At the root of this response is a misconception that rules the life of some individuals. This misconception states, "I am unable to be successful at anything." The reality is that these persons do not believe in themselves. In light of this, Marcus Garvey championed a very important concept — "If you have no confidence in self, you are twice defeated in the race of life. With confidence you have won even before you have started" (Garvey Memorial 2005 - Internet). This is central to the issue of believing in one's self, and crucial to one's self-esteem.

The tougher side of the coin is how such negative individuals handle criticism. The cognitive processes, guided by their belief system, cause them to interpret negative criticism in a self-destructive manner. Their internal dialogue says that they are incompetent and unable to succeed. In addition, they believe that people do not like them. In light of this, negative criticism tends to break these individuals instead of making them resolute to succeed in whatever they do.

In dealing with challenges, they become frustrated with even minor setbacks. They engage in linear thinking (one way thinking) instead of lateral thinking (looking at various solutions). They focus on the problem instead of possible solutions. They do not see themselves as being able to change challenges into opportunities. **To them challenges do not serve as springboards for creativity and innovation but as broken bridges to self-condemnation.** They do not believe that new opportunities can be created out of past failures and disappointments. Their mindset is so negative, they are totally destroyed by it.

The cancerous mind causes persons to have selective-amnesia. They try to wipe some things out of their minds but these continue to affect them subconsciously. Unfortunately such persons forget good experiences focusing only on bad experiences. It almost becomes a compulsion for them to focus on, and remember the negative things that have happened to them. It is important for such persons to understand that if they focus on the negatives, they will find they have more than they can handle; similarly, if they focus on the positives, they will discover more than they ever realized and accomplish more. "If we allow ourselves to dwell on negatives, on hurts, on mistreatments, we will be negative thinkers" (Carson 1992, 153). Bluntly stated, **an exclusive focus on the bad things that have happened is extremely dangerous to one's mental health and well-being.** The cancerous mind provides the impetus for persons to become frustrated with life and become passive (do nothing) in their so-called quest for answers, meaning and significance.

Some people are fearful of bringing certain things to their conscious mind because they are unprepared to deal with the consequences of such discoveries. They therefore "age-up" without "growing-up". They scapegoat their issues by keeping themselves busy in all kinds of different activities until the flood gate opens, and they do not even recognize where the water is coming from. It is paradoxical that when persons fail to deal with their issues they put themselves in a state of inertia. Inertia propels decay because the law of entropy affirms that things will get progressively worse unless energy is exerted. The word 'energy' comes from the Greek word "energon", which means to be in work. This suggests that **in order to prevent things from getting worse, a person**

must do something. The irony, however, according to Oliver et al (1997, 23) is that "everyone wants to be different, but few people want to change".

Persons are equipped with the capacity to engage in introspection. However, because of the cancerous mind of some persons, their introspection skills are lacking. This response is due to a faulty basis for personal reflection. William Backus (1994, 15) agrees with this in affirming that "by never addressing the "misbeliefs" that inform our self-talk, we become victims of circumstances, events, and painful emotions." It is, therefore, dangerous when persons do not tell themselves the truth about themselves but instead believe lies. In introspection, it is very important that persons know who they are, their God, their purpose and their destiny. Persons need to understand that they are wired for success and shaped for a purpose. Poor introspection causes individuals to sink deeper in the mire of self-recrimination and self-condemnation.

The danger that many people faced and have not been able to handle properly has to do with taking appropriate share of responsibility for what happened to them. It becomes dangerous when persons do not have a sense of personal responsibility or take too much of the responsibility. When persons take their appropriate share of the responsibility, it allows them to learn from negative experiences. **A sense of personal responsibility allows persons to grow through negative experiences**. It allows persons to rise above the role of victims and become victors.

The cancerous mind causes persons to form unlike parallels. They do not weigh each situation on its own merit or demerit but group one thing based on another. They do not move on from one experience into another experience successfully because they engage in self-defeating thoughts. They begin to engage in splitting. That is, something is either all good or all bad to them.

Some persons have a tendency to defeat themselves by beating themselves mentally. Their cancerous mind causes them to destroy themselves slowly. It is very frightening when learned, competent and brilliant persons have low self-concept and low self-esteem. The problem lies in the fact that their cancerous mind is not allowing them to believe in themselves.

The use of language, even internally, is very powerful. We use language to express ourselves to ourselves and to express ourselves to others. There are some words that dominate some people's vocabulary that they need to reject. The way they phrase their sentences is very important. For example, in complimenting someone, they say "That was not bad", instead of rating the person's performance on a positive scale. If something is good, then come right out and pronounce it as such. Say to the other person. "That is really good!" Some persons on the other hand have a habit of using words to destroy themselves not others. They also allow others to use words to destroy them. They need to learn how to reframe, reword, rethink, re-programme and redirect their cognitive processes or ways of thinking.

Others need to stop allowing themselves to operate on the force of their evil thoughts. **When people operate under the force of their evil thoughts, they do not look for the right way out but the easy way**. The truth is there is no quick fix for some of the human predicaments. "People who look for the easy way out seem to have trouble finding an exit" (Motivational Quotes 2005 - Internet). Their delusion operates like a ghastly cancer, eating away the substance of their existence. They become cowards on their life's pilgrimage, giving opportunity to the devil and others to control their lives with fear and a sense of helplessness and hopelessness. In addition, their locus of control becomes external instead of internal. That is, they give other people and things control over their lives.

> *Here is a case for reflection on the cancerous mind.* Ms C. grew up with her mother, father, brothers and sisters. Her father died when she was very young. She stopped going to school when she was fifteen years old because she did not pass the exam to go to high school. She decided to get vocational training, so she went to one of the Heart Trust Vocational Training Schools in Kingston, Jamaica. She did well in the school and graduated. Various companies employed her. She had to leave the last job because her boss was making sexual advances at her. She was trying to do some CXC subjects for many years but kept stopping because she did not believe in herself although she was doing well professionally. She had the opportunity to do an entrance examination and get into college but she was worried about not having any money. She would rather stay home and pay rent with all her savings than starting college and ask her family for help or just work hard for scholarships or seek a part-time job on campus. She was afraid to make the

move because she did not believe in herself. She did not think that she could do well academically.

The above case is a good illustration of how the cancerous mind works. It prevents a person from building on his/her small successes. Instead of making some effort, that is, taking little steps forward, the person stays in his/her "comfort zone". No effort is made in venturing out. Like Ms. C., it causes a person to tell himself/herself that he/she is unable to succeed because of where he/she is coming from. It allows a person to use the past to colour the future. As a result, a person makes his/her "corner" dark because of what he/she tells himself/herself.

Reflections

Confront the Cancerous Mind

1. Listen to your internal dialogue. What words dominate your thoughts especially as it relates to your goal and destiny?

   ....
   ....
   ....
   ....
   ....

2. What painful experience(s) have you had that you do not want to remember?

   ....
   ....
   ....
   ....
   ....

3. What do you want to change about yourself?

   ....
   ....
   ....
   ....
   ....

The Cancerous Heart

The condition of one's heart is very important. Some people have a gangrene cancerous heart. In this concept of the cancerous heart, the heart is seen as the seat of a person's inner life. It is the basis on which persons make moral judgment and moral decision. It is the basis on which persons construct principles to guide their lives. A person's heart guides the values and attitudes that he/she possesses. It is the basis on which an individual makes choices that are guided by values overtly or covertly held by him/her.

An individual's cancerous heart causes him/her to live by loose values. At times, he/she does not even understand the underlying principles that guide the things that he/she does. It is even more difficult to fathom when an individual does not know why he/she believes some of the things that he/she believes and have some of the attitudes that he/she possesses. Beliefs are very powerful, to the extent that it has been posited that it is potent enough to either kill or cure. The cancerous heart causes individuals to hold onto beliefs that are sucking out their life blood. Some of the beliefs are rooted in their family history and they are expected and coerced to uphold them either directly or indirectly. Some of them are rooted in learned behaviours from one's culture and society.

The cancerous heart eats away at the objective moral standards that persons should be living by and causes their consciences to become seared or hardened. It is absurd when persons do not know why they believe what they believe. They often become self-centred and in the process destroy their own lives. It mars critical thinking skills and moral judgment at all levels.

It becomes challenging for these persons to experience the appropriate range of emotions, even experiencing appropriate guilt. The cancerous mind coupled with the cancerous heart causes individuals to turn appropriate anger into aggression and violence. **Some persons hold onto beliefs that are destroying them**. They live by evil superstitions so they live in fear. Their values cause them to deal inappropriately with their emotions.

It is the beliefs of persons that keep them trapped in situations that are working against them. They are holding onto what they should let go. The perennial problem is that sometimes persons do not realize how deeply entrenched, de-motivating, damaging, dangerous and demonic some beliefs and values are. Remember, the devil is very deceptive. The cancerous heart and mind are holding some persons captives in the continuous dark night of their souls. They feel and believe that there is no way out for them because they are buried in the mire of devastating and troubling experiences which are etched on their minds. This wreaks havoc in their hearts and, therefore, conquer their lives. In short, these individuals lose total control of their lives.

It is painstakingly hurtful and hard to swallow when persons who are battered and bruised by various circumstances remain in that state because their beliefs and values continue to make them sink deeper in the mud. Persons need to challenge their values so that they can lift their lives to a higher standard. You have to engage in what Gerard Egan (2002, 219) calls 'self challenge', in order to change challenges into opportunities. What people believe about themselves, the world, the future or others becomes skewed in a self-destructive manner because of their cancerous heart. Their entire thought process is, unfortunately, warped.

Many individuals live unhealthy lives because of their values. Some of the things that they say do not match up with the things that they do. This is so because their deeply rooted values are not consciously stated in what they say at times. The actions of persons sometimes do not match their words. It is a strange and destructive state of affairs when such individuals deceive themselves. When thoughts conflict with action, the result is chaos.

The cancerous heart like the cancerous mind affects the education, relationships, career and every other area of people's lives. At times, some do not even believe in themselves. The cancerous heart of some has caused them to give the power of evil control over their lives. They become scared, fearful and afraid. The cancerous heart causes some persons to develop a pessimistic attitude towards life.

Often, people have a way of killing themselves with their thoughts and beliefs. In order for persons to release themselves from the gripping and teething effects of lies that abound in their belief system, they need to leave certain things that they have been cleaving to either consciously or unconsciously. It is only by dealing with the cancerous mind, that persons can acquire the skills and the power to deal with the cancerous heart, so that they can become hearty. It is worth noting that the cancerous mind and heart operate in tandem (together).

> **Here is a story for reflection on the cancerous heart**. One day I was at home. I heard this boy calling the next door neighbour. He kept on calling and calling. Nobody responded to him. The dogs were barking and he kept calling. I was studying and was very disturbed by his constant calling. When he did not get any answer, he went away. After a few minutes he came back. I was now outside hanging out some clothes. I was amused by his constant calling. This time he did not come up to the neighbours' gate, he stayed a little distance off. He continued to call. There was no response. After I was through hanging out the clothes, I went to him and asked "Why are you still calling, you do not see that nobody is there?" He responded, "But the door is open."

The above mentioned story is a good example of how the cancerous heart works. It causes a person to believe that he/she has control over the behaviour of other individuals. It allows a person to believe that he or she has control when it is not so. It makes it easy for a person to believe the false notion that things are always the way they seem and so they will get the answer that they are looking for, although they do not have control over the external factors.

Reflections

Confront the Cancerous Heart

1. What do you believe about yourself?

   ....
   ....
   ....
   ....

2. What things are you afraid of doing?

   ....
   ....
   ....
   ....
   ....
   ....

3. What causes you to be afraid of doing these things?

   ....
   ....
   ....
   ....

4. List all the things that you like about yourself (at least ten).

   ....
   ....
   ....
   ....
   ....
   ....
   ....
   ....
   ....

5. Look in the mirror and tell yourself that you are special because Jesus loves you and if you were the only one in the world He would still die for you. Do this three times per day. How does this make you feel at the end of the day?

   ....
   ....
   ....
   ....
   ....

6. Make a list of all your strengths.

   ....
   ....
   ....
   ....
   ....
   ....

7. Make a list of the good things that others have said about you.

   ....
   ....
   ....
   ....
   ....
   ....
   ....
   ....

8. Make a list of your important achievements.

   ....
   ....
   ....
   ....
   ....
   ....

The Cancerous Ear

The cancerous ear causes persons to hear what they want to hear. It causes them to engage in all forms of inappropriate listening. They get upset without even recognizing that they have not heard what was said. Some persons engage in destructive arguments because they have not heard clearly what was said. They are insecure and frail so they use all forms of defensive mechanisms feverishly trying to protect their image. The cancerous ear is geared at pushing people to protect their public image. The paradox is that it causes people to damage their public image. "He who answers before listening — that is his folly and shame" (Proverbs 18:13).

> ***Here is a case for reflection.*** *One morning Armstrong came to school early. When Dick arrived he saw Armstrong in the classroom with some other students. Dick called out, "Armstro…..ng". Armstrong and Dick got into a fight because Armstrong claimed that Dick disrespected him by telling him that his "arm is strong" (he has a bad body odour). Armstrong used a pen to stab Dick in his head. Dick had to be rushed to the hospital. A teacher came by and was concerned about Armstrong's attitude because there was no sense of remorse on his face or in his general attitude. The teacher said to Armstrong, "I do not like your attitude; you are behaving like a murderer." The boy started cursing and carrying on, saying that the teacher called him a murderer. The student was a peer counsellor and when his Form Teacher and Counsellor came they were shocked because the boy's behaviour was out of character.*

The cancerous ear is propelled by a person's cancerous heart and mind. It is very destructive when persons have a habit of hearing what they want to hear. This is, in fact, taking what has been said to them out of context. This causes conflicts to develop making conflict resolution very difficult. Persons with a cancerous ear are cantankerous and hard to get along with because they will not listen to others and complain that others are not listening to them, when they are the ones who are not listening. This is like an atomic bomb waiting to explode. The speaker accuses the listener for not listening. The cancerous ear causes persons to engage in the quest for audience unnecessarily. Such persons seek the approval of others to such an extent that it prevents persons accepting the truth because they refuse to hear the truth. It, therefore, can be argued that one's perception is distorted simply by taking such a biased position.

Reflections

1. Do you listen to what people have to say before you speak? Explain your answer.

   ....
   ....
   ....
   ....
   ....

2. What goes on in your mind when you feel threatened?

   ....
   ....
   ....
   ....
   ....

3. Do you have a compelling drive to protect yourself when you feel like you are being attacked? If so, how do you protect yourself?

   ....
   ....
   ....
   ....
   ....

4. When the speaker after receiving your verbal abuses respond, do you find him/her saying, "That is not what I said?" Explain your answer.

....
....
....
....
....

The Cancerous Eye

People have a tendency to put up smoke screens because they do not want to deal with their issues. They hide behind trivial concerns in order to escape their frightening realities. They turn a blind eye to their real issues hoping that they will go away. This is so because the cancerous eye causes tunnel and myopic vision. Persons have a tendency 'to stick out their eye' in accepting the wrong "i" by claiming ignorance, which leads to irresponsibility, which leads to inertia, which leads to indoctrination, which leads to intolerance, which leads to isolation, which leads to instability, which leads to internment (death).

Persons have a tendency to create what they want to see, especially the wrong thing. The cancerous eye causes them to muddy the water even much more and then try to discover answers. It causes them to walk in danger even without recognizing it. They live on the edge and do not even recognize that they are hanging over the precipice. They refuse to see the possible things they can do to live a successful life. It causes them to see the persons who have hurt them, not the road to recovery. It causes them to be unable to recognize where they are. For healing to take place, persons must recognize where they are. They need to be able to see where they are and to examine what they can do to recover from the aftermath of their dark experiences of suffering.

The paradox is that if individuals are unable to see, they are unable to make proper assessment and move on successfully. The cancerous eye must be healed; the scale must fall off people's eyes. Seeing and hearing what one wants to see and hear are usually unconscious acts of which one is unaware until someone confronts him/her with his/her failure to hear and see what needs to be heard and seen. When the confrontation takes place, it is usually painful and denied. Help, hope, and change can only come when the confrontation is accepted and the cancerous ears and eyes are transformed.

Reflections

1. What are you seeing as you reflect on your life?

   ....
   ....
   ....
   ....
   ....
   ....
   ....
   ....
   ....

2. What would you love to see that you are not currently seeing?

   ....
   ....
   ....
   ....
   ....
   ....
   ....
   ....
   ....

3. Visualize what you want to see by creating it in the mind. How does this make you feel about yourself?

....
....
....
....
....
....
....
....

4. Believe what you visualized, pray about it and work to achieve it. Do you believe that if you can conceive it, you can achieve it by God's grace? Provide reasons for your answer.

....
....
....
....
....
....

The Cancerous Feet and Hands

The cancerous feet cause persons to walk through life aimlessly. Such persons tell themselves that they are unable to move forward so they remain passive. They probably have been told that they will not come out to anything good. They become entangled in a vicious cycle of self-crucifixion. They put limits on how far they can go because of the lies that they believe. They operate like a car that has been made to travel at 200 kilometres an hour but being driven at 80 kilometres an hour because of the law of the land. Toll road was introduced allowing persons to travel at 110 kilometres an hour but the driver is afraid to travel at 110 kilometres an hour because he/she is accustomed to travelling at 80 kilometres an hour. **The cancerous feet make persons afraid to try out new behaviours**. It causes persons to keep doing the same thing while wishing to get different results.

> *Here is a case story for reflection — (Anonymous).*
>
> **'Born to Fly'** *One day a prairie chicken found an egg and sat on it until it hatched. Unbeknownst to the prairie chicken, the egg was an eagle egg, abandoned for some reason. That was how an eagle came to be born into a family of prairie chickens.*
>
> *While the eagle is the greatest of all birds, soaring above the heights with grace and ease, the prairie chicken does not even know how to fly. In fact, prairie chickens are so lowly that they eat garbage.*
>
> *Predictably, the little eagle, being raised in a family of prairie chickens, thought he was a prairie chicken. He walked around, ate garbage, and clucked like a prairie chicken.*
>
> *One day he looked up to see a majestic bald eagle soar through the air, dipping and turning. When he asked his family what it was, they responded, "It's an eagle. But you could never be like that because you are just a prairie chicken." Then they returned to pecking the garbage.*
>
> *The eagle spent his whole life looking up at eagles, longing to join them among the clouds. It never once occurred to him to lift his wings and try to fly. The eagle died thinking he was just a prairie chicken.*

You might be told that you cannot do something. Ignore this negative feedback and follow your inner drive. Those who are giving you information might not know your true potential. **Do not allow your dream to die by sharing it with the wrong persons**. Do not just wish for things to happen; try out your wings; they have the capacity to take you where you want to go. Do not just look at where you want to be, get rid of the cancerous feet; do something. John Gray (2004, xvi), agrees with this concept by affirming that "one small but significant change can have a lasting and dramatic impact."

The cancerous feet encourage laziness. Persons sit back and do nothing because they say it is not their fault why they are who they are. They would prefer to die rather than try to help themselves. This is what I call the 'Jonah attitude'. They become stuck in the mud because they are afraid of leaving a hole behind. They would rather be stuck than having to look back at the hole where they have been. The paradox is that they become fearful instead of careful. **Ironically, some persons hold onto straws claiming that they want to get out knowing that the straws are not strong enough to help them out**. That is, they choose to do the things that will not work because they are afraid to deal with the pain that their problems have mushroomed into. They allow things to happen instead of doing what needs to be done to make what they want to happen, happen. The cancerous feet cause people to go to places that sink them deeper, not lift them higher.

The cancerous feet propel inertia. If an individual fails to act, he acts to fail. It is easy to be easy. It takes effort to be active; being easy when you should be active can have devastating consequences. **It behoves every one to break inertia by exerting energy to stop the collision course that he/she is on with disaster**. Human beings are privileged to be privileged and so should not abuse their privileges.

The cancerous hands causes persons to do things that are destructive to themselves and others. Sometimes they become hard in the way they deal with others. They displace their anger and make life frustrating for others. They become very active in helping others and neglect themselves. They sometimes end up doing the same things to others that they abhorred being meted out to them. They become undisciplined and infantile in their behaviours. The cancerous hands and feet of persons, therefore, cause serious interpersonal problems. Such individuals go through life engaging in meaningless work. They merely strive to endure life not enjoy life. Thus, they even become passively aggressive. That is, they do not do things that they can do. They do things that they should not do because they want to get back at others, thinking it will hurt those who have hurt them. This revenge borne of wrong thinking achieves the exact opposite. The person bent on revenge will self-destruct himself/herself.

The cancerous state of some persons causes them to live their lives in a non-assertive mood. That is to say, they have a lot of "ifs" and "buts." The ghastly cancerous heart, mind, feet, ear, hand and eye make it extremely difficult for people to extricate themselves from themselves and to tear themselves from the external forces that are waging war against their freedom to be who they were created to be. People can only release themselves from the negative impact of life experiences by freeing themselves from self bondage so that they can free themselves from the bad experiences that they went through.

> ***Here is a case for reflection****. The story is told of a couple who went to the Registrars General's Department in Jamaica to get their marriage certificate. After years of searching for the record, nothing was found. The grown children of the couple were very concerned. One of the children came from overseas and visited the Registrars General's Department with her mother. The director interviewed the mother. She asked her, who performed the ceremony? She said "Nobody was there; it was just me and my husband. I went and bought a ring and prepared a nice meal and when my children's father came from the field, he bathed and put on nice clothes and put the ring on my finger and married me." The lady confessed after all of that, they did not want their children to know that they were not officially married.*

The above is a very good illustration of the cancerous feet and hand. Like the couple, individuals know that what they are doing and where they are going will not bring about the result that they are seeking but they continue nevertheless. The couple knew that no information was sent to the Registrars General's Department but they were still going there expecting to get something. The cancerous feet and hand cause persons to move in a particular direction and do things, not to get results but to save face. Such persons end up losing face in the long-term. Reality cannot be faked, it exists and has to be faced squarely.

Reflections

1. What are you currently doing that is working against you?

   ....
   ....
   ....
   ....
   ....
   ....
   ....
   ....
   ....

2. Do you think you are behaving like the eagle that thought it was a prairie chicken? Explain your answer.

   ....
   ....
   ....
   ....
   ....
   ....
   ....
   ....
   ....
   ....
   ....

3. What do you need to do differently to get what you want and fulfil your purpose?

....
....
....
....
....
....
....
....
....
....
....

CHAPTER 4
Emotional Consequences of Issues Faced

In this section, the emphasis is placed on the emotional consequences that are experienced as a result of negative experiences. It seeks to help you to understand the importance of accepting and working through your emotions. Careful attention is given to the ways in which emotions manifest themselves if they are not properly dealt with. Attention is also called to some emotions that you need to be aware of because you might be experiencing them based on your past experiences. The Reflections are geared at helping you to identify your emotions, own them, and process them.

It is important for you to be in touch with your feelings so that you can process them for your health and healing to take place. God has created you with emotions to protect yourself as well as to enjoy yourself. In the same way that you are able to experience physical pain and pleasure, you also have the capacity to experience emotional pain and pleasure. As a result of how lavishly human beings are endowed with emotions by God, one author argued that we are "millionaires in emotions in combination and intensity" (Lutzer 1983, 13). God has given you emotions and He is able to give you the strength to deal with them and heal those that need to be healed.

Emotions are placed in two categories: those that are pleasurable and those that are painful. "Emotions are defined as changes in arousal levels that may either interfere with or facilitate motivated behaviour" (Turner and Helms 1995, 220). This is a good definition of emotions because it clearly suggests that emotions affect our actions. The way you feel is brought about by the things that you experienced and your thoughts about those things can either be conscious or unconscious.

It is important for you to feel anger towards those who have hurt you because underneath your anger is the pain, hurt, loss and betrayal that you are experiencing. There are six basic emotions. "The three pleasant emotions are happiness, excitement, and tenderness. The three protective emotions are sadness, scare [fear], and anger" (Stutzman and Schrock-Shenk 1995, 72). Anger, one of the protective emotions, helps to protect you from further hurt and warns you that something is wrong that you need to work through.

There are a lot of silent tears that persons are crying because of various forms of abuse and other negative experiences suffered. **It is very difficult to deal with emotional pain which can come from a variety of sources**. John Gray (2004, 263), sees anger, sadness, fear, and regret as the four primary aspects of emotional pain. The silent tears keep going because persons are afraid to talk about the hurt and pain that they are going through. In addition, persons do not want to admit the hurt and pain that they are experiencing. In order to stop the tears, you must own your emotions and process them. According to David G. Benner (2003, 89), "feelings that are avoided are empowered." That is, if you do not deal with your negative emotions, they get stronger. This is so because our emotions affect us consciously or unconsciously. **It is very easy to project our unresolved feelings onto others, which is destructive to building and maintaining healthy relationships**. John Gray (2004, 311) agrees with this in his assertion that, "when we are upset, about 90 percent of the upset is related to our past and has nothing to do with what we think is upsetting us." This underscores the importance for us to resolve the issues in our lives.

The emotions that are experienced have to do with the meaning that is attached to the situation experienced. There is an approach to counselling known as logotherapy which seeks to explore this issue of meaning (Ivey and Ivey 1999, 275). **You need to objectively give the right meaning to the negative experiences that you have had**. This is necessary for proper processing of your experiences. Don't deny your emotions. **Validate your feelings so you can work through them**.

The "Graved" Emotions

In this concept of "graved" emotions, the emphasis is on how negative emotions manifest themselves in a person's life. Grave is used in reference to how the emotions are placed in the "tomb" or buried. This is facilitated by the cancerous heart. There are three kinds of ways that negative emotions manifest themselves in a person's life. Firstly, there is the covered grave. This refers to pent up emotions, emotions that are held in check and not expressed or discussed. This is like retreating into what Mulholland (1993, 87) calls a "protective cocoon." **Persons with "graved" emotions lie about their true feelings in an attempt to protect themselves**. There is a façade that penetrates these persons' entire lives. That is, they go around behaving like they are happy when, in fact, they are broken and torn. So, in reality, the loudest laughter is a camouflage for the tears inside. A truly happy person is serene for he/she has the peace that passes all understanding that the Bible speaks of.

When you try to protect yourself, it results in you hurting yourself and potentially hurting others. There is, therefore, a very important need for you to release pent-up emotions. Pent-up emotions can be released through a process known as catharsis. That is, by talking to a skilled counsellor, a confidant, journaling or prayer. This need for catharsis is supported by Gerald Corey (2000, 120), who articulated that, "keeping a lid on anger, pain, frustration, hatred, and fear means preventing spontaneous feelings such as joy, affection, delight, and enthusiasm from emerging." Please note that in order to release pent-up emotions, at times professional help must be sought.

Secondly, there is the uncovered grave. This refers to negative emotions that are allowed to dominate a person's life. These emotions are evident in the person's mood, facial expression and action. These persons are very grumpy and love to deny that they are hurting.

Finally, there is the grave-less emotions. These emotions are very pervasive. These persons are not afraid to talk about their bad experiences and the subsequent hurt and pain that they are feeling. However, they have not processed their emotions. They just accept them as a part of life. They end up just coping with life instead of enjoying life. In talking about their hurt and pain, they deceive themselves by telling themselves that they have gotten over it. Those who work with them can easily see that they are just trying to exist, not existing to fulfil their purpose.

It is important to admit your emotions. Accept that you are angry, hurt, and confused. This is important for healing to take place. Be aware, of and accept your emotions. **Your emotional scars can be healed**. "Christ came to heal and redeem our damaged emotions as well as our souls" (Kirwan 1984, 42).

It is important to be able to recognize and name emotions. Healthy hearts, not cancerous hearts, are able to experience a range of emotions in a healthy manner. "To heal our inner pain, we must feel each of the four primary aspects of emotional pain. They are anger, sadness, fear, and regret" (Gray 2004, 263). Here are some other important emotions that you might need to identify, admit and process based on your past negative experiences:

- Feeling of worthlessness - "when children are ignored or excessively criticized, they begin to feel worthless" (Collins 1988, 95).
- Feeling weak
- Feeling shy
- Feeling ashamed
- Feeling afraid
- Feeling unaccepted
- Feeling lonely
- Feeling rejected
- Feeling dejected
- Feeling unattractive
- Feeling anxious — anxiety distorts thinking (Wachtel and Messer 1997, 57).
- Feeling hopeless
- Feeling helpless
- Feeling let-down
- Feeling abandoned
- Feeling dirty
- Feeling a sense of guilt
- Feeling powerless

Here is a very important caution. **Don't wait until you feel how you want to feel before you do what you need to do.** Charles Allen Kollar

(1997, 125) suggests that "feelings may change if you act differently." According to the cognitive behavioural approach to this book, in order to act differently you have to change your thinking. Another important thing that you can do is "pick and choose which thoughts you wish to react to" (Carlson 1997, 22). That is, do not focus on your negative thoughts or feeling.

Reflections

1. Ask some persons to guess how you are feeling. Write down their responses.

   ....
   ....
   ....
   ....
   ....
   ....

2. How many persons guessed correctly?

   ....
   ....
   ....
   ....
   ....

3. What does this say about the need to express your emotions or feelings?

   ....
   ....
   ....
   ....
   ....

4. How do you feel most of the time?

   ....
   ....
   ....
   ....
   ....
   ....
   ....
   ....

5. Can these feelings be objectively justified? Explain your answer.

   ....
   ....
   ....
   ....
   ....
   ....
   ....
   ....

6. How do you plan to change your negative feelings? Write out a plan.

   ....
   ....
   ....
   ....
   ....
   ....
   ....
   ....

PART II

PART II

Creating A New Self

Here is a continuation of the story about the eagle started in Part I. One day, a veterinarian came by to do some work for the farmer. The farmer started boasting about the big chicken that he has. The veterinarian went and looked at the farmer's big chicken and told the farmer that it is an eagle, not a chicken. The farmer did not believe him. The farmer said, "I raised it like a chicken and it is behaving like a chicken, it is a chicken."

The veterinarian said to the farmer, "let me prove to you that it is an eagle". The veterinarian took the eagle and threw it in the air and it fell. The farmer laughed and said, "I told you that it is a chicken." The veterinarian tried again and the same thing happened.

The veterinarian went away and came back the following day. He said to the eagle, "You are not a chicken; you are an eagle, you can fly." The farmer still kept saying it is a chicken. The veterinarian threw the eagle in the air and it flew a little and came down. The veterinarian believed in the eagle's ability to fly so he continued to work with the eagle until the eagle flew away to the surprise of the farmer.

The remainder of this story illustrates how sometimes people do not believe in their God-given potential. It also shows that **there is no quick fix for some of our human predicaments but they can be fixed**. Therefore, a new self-understanding will emerge when you process your current self-understanding. Change your thoughts and beliefs which are working against you. Recognize that "the biggest inhibition to change lies within yourself, and that nothing gets better until you change" (Johnson 1998, 72). Stop believing lies about yourself and start believing the truth.

It is very important for you to find the courage to accept yourself to move past your pain. Reject your current self-understanding and embrace the fact that you are special regardless of your past experiences. You are wired for success and shaped for a purpose. **God can use your strengths as well as your scars in the process of allowing you to fulfil your purpose in life**. Your Creator designed you for a purpose and has equipped you with the tools to achieve your destiny.

A new self-understanding causes you to see yourself as a work in progress. You have not arrived but you are getting there. Tell yourself that you are willing to do whatever it takes to get there. Believe in your God-given potential. See yourself as having the capacity to become all that God wants you to become.

Your new self-understanding will cause you to see yourself as broken but not paralysed. You are broken because you have the capacity to feel the hurt and pain that you have suffered. However, you are not paralysed. You have the capacity to process and handle feelings constructively. God has given you the strength to deal with your scars. Your scars can become a part of the tool that God uses to help others to gain strength. Even that which seems bad can be put to good use. Remember, a scar, rather than an open wound, indicates healing has taken place. **God uses "broken vessels" like you and moulds them into "vessels of honour"**. Remember, that is you — a "vessel of honour".

In this section, the focus is on creating a new self. The focus in Chapter 5 will be placed on truth about you from your Creator's perspective. In Chapter 6, the focus is placed on you being a master fighter, which is based on the fact that as a person you are very resilient. In Chapter 7, the focus will be on you as a keen individual; you are able to maximize your potential.

CHAPTER 5

Truths About Self

In this section, the focus is placed on you creating a new self by understanding the truths about yourself from the perspective of your Creator. It focuses on the fact that you are special regardless of your past. In addition, it is demonstrated that you can enjoy your life regardless of what you have been through. The Reflections aim at helping you to see yourself from your Creator's perspective and accept yourself for who you really are.

Truth Number One - I Am Special

You are special because you were created by God in His image and likeness, like all other human beings (Genesis 1:31). However, there is just one you. God took the time to make you into who you are. He makes no junk. You are special. **No matter what occasioned your birth, God conceived you before you were conceived (Isaiah 44:2).** This is the truth about you and a lie cannot stand up in the face of truth. **Truth resonates with us, empowers and liberates us**. I am saying here that you need to allow this truth to penetrate your entire being and liberate you. The truth is what will set you free from the damaging, destructive, demonic, de-motivating, dark and deadly lies that you have come to believe about yourself. "God doesn't want us just to know who we are in Him; He wants us to become it" (Munroe 1996, 67). This is ultimately the reason why truth empowers and liberates.

You are so special that God not only created you but He gave you responsibilities (Genesis 2:19). He knows you better than everyone and even better than you know yourself because He created you. He knew that you were capable of carrying out the responsibilities that He gave you. The Creator of the world has given you responsibilities. Wow! You are special.

He not only created you and gave you responsibilities He also gave you restrictions (Genesis 2:16, 17). He gave you restrictions because He wants the best for you. You are so special and that is why He wants to have a close relationship with you.

God rescued you so that it is possible for you to have this close relationship with Him. This was necessary as a result of the broken relationship that was brought about by the disobedience of Adam and Eve. He loves you so much that He gave the life of His only begotten Son for you (John 3:16). He wants you to have abundant life. He wants your life to be meaningful and significant. You are valuable; you are worth the life of God's only begotten Son. You are very special. You were given the ability by God to reason and choose (Genesis 2:19; 2:16, 17). You are not inferior or superior; you are unique (Psalm 8:3-8). God says that you are precious and honoured in His sight because He loves you (Isaiah 43:4).

God is establishing you in every area of your life if you have accepted His love. He is working all things together for your good, that is, to make you more like Jesus (Romans 8:28, 29). He is doing this to fulfil His purpose for your life (Jeremiah 29:11). Therefore, you can maximize your potential. You can do all things through Christ who is strengthening you (Philippians 4:13). This suggests that when God is working in you and you are working out your salvation with fear and trembling before Him, you can declare like Paul, "I can do all things in Christ who strengthens me" (Philippians 4:13). **You can get past your past because God is working on you.** You can deal with your hurt and pain because God is empowering you. Your God is faithful. You can establish good relationships. You can develop a new mind-set and belief system.

In developing a new mind-set and belief system, you need to reflect on your worldview. You need to clarify your worldview, what Stanley and Markman (1999, 115) call core beliefs and values. This is important because your worldview influences your life and relationships in every way. What God says about you must become the foundation of your worldview.

Sin has affected every area of your life inclusive of social, emotional, mental, psychological, relational, biological, spiritual and developmental. However, healing is available in Jesus Christ. When you surrender to God by believing Jesus died and rose again for you and invite Him into your heart and life, you will be confident that He has begun a good work in you and He will bring it to completion (Philippians 1:6). **With God working on you and you playing your part, you can be healed from your past hurt, pain and betrayal**. You are a work in progress. You can become all that God has created you to become. **It is our God-confidence that gives us true self-confidence**.

> **Reflect on this quotation from Marcus Garvey**: *The...man or woman who has no confidence in self is an unfortunate being, and is really a misfit in creation. God Almighty created earth and every one of us for a place in the world, and for the least of us to think that we were created only to be what we are and not what we can make ourselves, is to impute an improper motive to the Creator for creating us..."* ***(Sacred Service 2005 - Internet)***

Truth Number Two — I Can Enjoy My Life
It is possible for you to enjoy your life by understanding the following:
1. Understanding the root of your problem: the fallen state of the world and your own personal sin
2. Understanding God's ultimate purpose for your life — (John 3:16)
3. Understanding your destiny: an appointment with death and judgment (Job 14:1; Ecclesiastes 3:2; 11:14; Hebrews. 9:27)
4. Surrendering your life to Jesus (1 John 1:9)

EXPLANATION
1. You are not the master of your own fate. God is sovereign over your life and you are ultimately responsible to Him. You will have to give an account to Him for the way that you have used the resources with which He has blessed you.
2. Is the way that you have structured your life working for you? It is important to emphasize that you cannot be made whole and thus be healed outside of Christ. In Christ you will find wholesome and lasting change. In Him you will spiral towards total re-creation as you yield to Him by doing what He requires of you. If the way that you have structured your life is not working for you, it means that you need to make some adjustments by letting Jesus Christ into your heart so He can control your life.
3. You might be asking, where is God in all of the things that you are going

through? He is establishing you. "God is involved with us in the most imprisoning bondage of our brokenness" (Mulholland 1993, 37).
4. Your true identity is in God. You were created in His own image and likeness. He knows who you are. You are special.
5. You were created with the capacity to enjoy relationship with God and man.
6. God wants you to be sanctified. He wants you to be like Christ. He wants to dwell in you so that He can control your life. When He is controlling your life, you are able to pursue excellence under divine direction. If you want to accept Jesus Christ, here is your Romans road to Christ:

1. Romans 3:23 - For all have sinned and fall short of the glory of God,
2. Romans 5:8 - But God demonstrated his own love for us in that: while we were still sinners, Christ died for us.
3. Romans 5:19 - For as through the disobedience of the one man the many were made sinners, so also through the obedience of the one man the many will be made righteous.
4. Romans 6:23 - For the wages of sin is death, but the gift of God is eternal life in Jesus Christ our Lord.
5. Romans 8:1 - Therefore, there is now no condemnation for those who are in Christ Jesus,
6. Romans 10:9 - That if you confess with your mouth, "Jesus is Lord," and believe in your heart that God raised him from the dead, you will be saved.
7. Romans 12:1, 2 - Therefore, I urge you, brothers, in view of God's mercy, to offer your bodies as living sacrifices, holy and pleasing to God — this is your spiritual act of worship. Do not conform any longer to the pattern of this world, but be transformed by the renewing of your mind. Then you will be able to test and approve what God's will is — his good, pleasing and perfect will.

Challenge Yourself With Truth and Accept Yourself

You interpreted the terrible experiences you have gone through in such a way that you believe that you are dirty, worthless, good for nothing or incapable of achieving your goals. You tell yourself that you cannot get over your past. However, sometimes you tell yourself that you have gotten over it when you know that you have not dealt with it successfully.

You believe the lies that persons have told you about yourself, for example, that you are worthless and nothing good is going to emanate from your life. You believe that you are the worst person in the world and deserve to die. You believe that the only way to get over your past is by committing suicide. That is, you believe that things would be better if you were dead. This is a lie because no matter how dreadful your experiences have been, you can work them through in order to fulfil your God-given purpose. The aforementioned can be illustrated by the following email that a friend sent me (the author is unknown).

* * * * * *

The Fern and the Bamboo

One day I decided to quit... I quit my job, my relationship, my spirituality ... I wanted to quit my life. I went to the woods to have one last talk with God. "God", I said. "Can you give me one good reason not to quit?"

His answer surprised me... "Look around", He said. "Do you see the fern and the bamboo?" "Yes", I replied.

> "When I planted the fern and the bamboo seeds, I took very good care of them. I gave them light. I gave them water. The fern quickly grew from the earth. Its brilliant green covered the floor. Yet nothing came from the bamboo seed.
>
> But I did not quit on the bamboo. In the second year the fern grew more vibrant and plentiful. And again, nothing came from the bamboo seed. But I did not quit on the bamboo.
>
> "In the third year, there was still nothing from the bamboo seed. But I would not quit. In the fourth year, again, there was nothing from the bamboo seed. I would not quit." He said.
>
> "Then in the fifth year a tiny sprout emerged from the earth. Compared to the fern it was seemingly small and insignificant...But just six months later the bamboo rose to over 100 feet tall. It had spent the five years growing roots. Those roots made it strong and gave it what it needed to survive. I would not give any of my

creations a challenge it could not handle."
He said to me, "Did you know, my child, that all this time you have been struggling, you have actually been growing roots; "I would not quit on the bamboo. I will never quit on you."

"Don't compare yourself to others." He said. "The bamboo had a different purpose than the fern. Yet, they both make the forest beautiful. Your time will come", God said to me. "You will rise high!"

"How high should I rise?" I asked. "How high will the bamboo rise?" He asked in return.

"As high as it can?" I questioned. "Yes", He said, "Give me glory by rising as high as you can." I left the forest and brought back this story.

* * * * * *

You believe that if you forgive the person(s) who have hurt you, you must reconcile with him/her. This is a faulty concept because forgiveness does not mean reconciliation. **When you forgive appropriately, not cheap forgiveness, you must not put yourself at risk to be hurt again**. You may also believe that you cannot forgive. This is not true because you can and should offer appropriate forgiveness for your own health and healing.

You may believe that you are the cause of your hurt and pain because God is punishing you. Know that you are only responsible for your actions and God does not tempt any one with evil.

You may believe that you cannot establish meaningful relationships because of your past experiences. However, you can learn to establish healthy relationships if you are willing to take the risk of working through your hurt and pain. You can be healed from the devastating effects of the traumas that you have experienced. **Remember, it is not where you are now but where you can be that matters**. But make sure that you follow God's guidance and will and not your own will.

You may tell yourself that things will not get better. This is not true because life is filled with changes and challenges, which produce opportunities. You cannot prevent changes from taking place, but you can do what is in your power to make what you want to happen, happen. **You**

have the power by God's grace to turn your life in a positive direction.

You may tell yourself that nobody loves you. This is not true because Jesus loves you. You are special because if you were the only person in this world Jesus would still die for you. You are so loved that He has engraved your name in the palm of His hand.

There is confusion on the issue of whether a person loves himself/herself or accepts himself/herself. The problem is not with persons loving themselves. Jesus and Scripture never tell us to love ourselves; it is a given (see Matthew 19:19; 23:39; Mark 12:31 & 33; Luke 10:27). Jesus urged His followers to love others as they love themselves. People who refuse to make necessary life changes because it is too painful, actually they love themselves too much and so avoid the pain necessary for healthy and responsible change. They are like the parent who says, "I love my child too much to discipline (spank) him/her." The fact of the matter is they love themselves too much to do what is necessary for the child's well-being.

The problem, therefore, is with self-acceptance, not self-love. Self-acceptance means that you own the good and the bad, the pleasurable and the painful, and integrate them into your life so as to be a better person because of both, rather than running from the painful. The challenge is for you to accept yourself and work at possessing and cultivating your "wealth of undiscovered and underdeveloped strengths, assets, and resources" (Clinebell 1984, 29).

You may tell yourself that you cannot accept yourself for who you are because of all the negative things that have happened to you. However, regardless of your past experiences you are special. **Accept yourself with your strengths and your scars and your treasures and tears**. If you do not first accept yourself, how do you expect others to accept you? Accept yourself for who you are as you work through overcoming your past in order to be who you were created to be by God. **Your strengths as well as your scars are shaping you for your God-given purpose**. "The difficulties of life are intended to make us better, not bitter" (Motivational Quotes 2005 - Internet).

Reflections

A Closer Look at Myself

1. List all the things that make you special according to your Creator (in His Word, the Bible).

   ....
   ....
   ....
   ....
   ....
   ....
   ....
   ....
   ....

2. Do you believe what your Creator said about you? Why or why not?

   ....
   ....
   ....
   ....
   ....
   ....
   ....
   ....
   ....

3. The Apostle Paul wrote, "I can do all things through Christ who strengthens me." List several ways this same attitude would help you in passing your past.

....
....
....
....
....
....
....
....
....
....
....
....
....
....

4. Building on what God said to Moses, "I am what I am," someone once said, "If I am says I am, then I am." Do you believe that if God says you are special you are special? Why or why not?

....
....
....
....
....
....
....
....
....
....
....
....
....

5. Are you at the point where you want to have a personal relationship with God or deepen or renew your commitment to Him? Why or why not?

   ....
   ....
   ....
   ....
   ....
   ....
   ....
   ....

6. If you were given an opportunity to look back at your life at the end, what would you want to change, even now?

   ....
   ....
   ....
   ....
   ....
   ....
   ....

8. Develop a plan to change what can be changed?

   ....
   ....
   ....
   ....
   ....
   ....
   ....

9. Develop a new perspective regarding what cannot be changed?

....
....
....
....
....
....
....
....

CHAPTER 6

Master Fighter

In this section, the focus is placed on you creating a new self by understanding that you are capable of taking hold of your life. You have the God-given potential to turn challenges into opportunities. You are resilient; you can accomplish your God-given purpose regardless of your past hurt, pain and betrayal. This section seeks to encourage and remind you that you have the right to fight to fulfil your God-given purpose and maximize your potential. The Reflections are geared at helping you to deal with the negatives in your life in the process of fulfilling your God-given purpose.

Find the courage to accept yourself with your pain of the past and the knowledge that God loves you and He can use your pain for your good that will enable you to pass your pain. This is necessary in your quest for meaning and significance. Regardless of what has happened to you, accept yourself. It is this acceptance of yourself that is going to enable you to work through those bad experiences in order to accomplish the God-given purpose for your life.

Refuse to be held captive by your past hurt and pain. Develop an internal locus of control. That is, determine to take responsibility for your life and control your thoughts, feelings and actions. Clyde M. Narramore (1960, 89) affirms the importance of internal control by positing that, "controls from within are truly the best ones because they do not require continual assistance from other people." Your internal control and motivation will cause you to work through the negatives in your life. Although your experiences can cause you to have regrets and feelings of shame, anger and guilt, remember that even though you have scars, you also have a lot of strengths. Your God-given potential is the source of your strengths. **You are wired for success and shaped for a purpose by the Almighty God**. Here are some guidelines to help you deal with the negatives in your life:

1. Accept the negatives if they are true.
2. See the negatives as challenges for you to grow.
3. Make a concerted effort to work on the negatives.
4. Become accountable to someone who will help you to work on the negatives.
5. Try to be an eternal optimist.
6. Remember, your thoughts affect your feeling. "What we too often fail to recognize is the connection between our feelings, our thoughts, and the ongoing internal monologue we carry on with ourselves at all times" (Backus 1994, 14). This asserts that you must exercise control over your thoughts in order to control your feelings.

You can work through the negatives in your life regardless of how challenging they are. As black people, we are very resilient. "Resilient persons can handle both deflation and inflation, both criticism and praise…" (Taylor 1989, 35). This reinforces the fact that you can deal with whatever comes your way. Our ancestors did not passively accept slavery but some of them fought while others tried to run away. After emancipation, they worked hard to build their lives. Marcus Garvey, one of Jamaica's National Heroes, because of his recognition of our resilience as black people declared, "Up you mighty race, you can accomplish what you will" (Simpson 2002, 21).

Marcus Garvey also charged us black people to emancipate ourselves from mental slavery. This is a vital recognition of the power of the mind. **Never allow your mind to hold you captive**. Free yourself and live like you are free. You are an eagle. Do not let any one treat you like a chicken. Do not be comfortable to roam on the ground when you have the capacity to soar high in the sky. The path before you might be challenging, but you can accomplish what God has created you to be and do. You are an eagle, not a chicken. Focus on the truth about yourself, not the lies that you have been told, which you have come to accept. Fight for that which truly belongs to you — your God-given potential and purpose.

Reflections

1. Make a list of all the things that you do not like about yourself.

   ....
   ....
   ....
   ....
   ....
   ....
   ....
   ....
   ....
   ....
   ....
   ....

2. Make a list of all the negative things that others have said about you.

   ....
   ....
   ....
   ....
   ....
   ....
   ....
   ....
   ....
   ....

3. Make a list of all the negative things that you believe about yourself.

   ....
   ....
   ....
   ....
   ....
   ....
   ....

4. Can the negative things pass the Biblical and objective tests? Why or why not?

   ....
   ....
   ....
   ....
   ....
   ....
   ....
   ....

5. God is able to turn your weaknesses into strengths. Do you believe this? Why or why not?

   ....
   ....
   ....
   ....
   ....
   ....
   ....

6. "I am a work in progress." Explain what this means.

   ....
   ....
   ....
   ....
   ....
   ....
   ....
   ....

7. "I am an eagle not a chicken"; what does this mean to you?

   ....
   ....
   ....
   ....
   ....
   ....
   ....
   ....

8. I am resilient; what does this mean to you?

   ....
   ....
   ....
   ....
   ....
   ....
   ....
   ....

9. I can accomplish what God wills for me by His grace; what does this mean to you?

   ....
   ....
   ....
   ....
   ....
   ....
   ....
   ....

CHAPTER 7

Keen Individual

In this section, the focus is placed on you creating a new self by understanding that you can become whatever God has designed for you to become. It is a part of your stewardship responsibility to become what you were created to be. You need to see yourself as a person who is zealous and eager to achieve the best. As a result, you are willing to do the possible to fulfil your God-given potential. Ten principles are examined and the reflections geared at helping you to develop a strategic plan to help you maximize your potential and fulfil your God-given purpose.

You are a person who is zealous to achieve the best. You are serious about maximising your potential and fulfilling your purpose. Regardless of your past, you are committed to be the best. This is how you should view yourself. You have refused to see yourself as a victim because you have stopped volunteering for that role. You have taken on the role of a victor because you want to maximize your potential.

It has become increasingly important for you to recognize that as a human being you must strive to be the best that you can be by God's grace. Strive to maximize your potential in this technological and informational age so that you will be poised to make a difference at various levels. The path to maximizing your potential is an active process. My wife reminded me that in a cartoon when the characters need strength beyond their ordinary power, they would say, "transformers activate". In like manner, learn to speak to your potential. To speak to your potential means to declare and decree in the name of Jesus what you want to be, and it will be fulfilled. God says, "Ask of me". Stop complaining about lack of resources and inadequacies. According to Maxwell and Dornan (1997, 52), "For most people, it's not what they are that holds them back. It's what they think they're not."

Therefore, get rid of negative thoughts or 'cancerous' activities. Be good stewards of your time, talents, abilities, gifts, resources and treasures. It is important that you strive to maximize your potential, all for the Glory of your Creator. Let us now examine ten principles to help you maximize your potential and fulfil your purpose.

1. Honour The Lord and He Will Honour You.

God has created us for Himself. That is, He wants us to have a personal relationship with Him. We must honour Him. Solomon instructs "Remember your Creator in the days of your youth, before days of trouble come and the years approach when you will say, "I have no pleasure in them" (Ecclesiastes 12:1). This suggests that God must come first. Jesus Christ instructs us to seek God first (Matthew 6:33). When you are honouring God, it means that your delight is in Him. "Delight yourself in the Lord and he will give you the desires of your heart" (Psalm 37:4). Doing that which God expects brings forth blessings. When your delight is in the Lord your desires will be pure and holy. When your desires are pure and holy, God will grant you your desires according to His will. Please note that striving for excellence is a part of honouring God.

It is a temptation for persons to believe that they can succeed without obeying God. This is a false concept of success for two reasons. Firstly, God's laws and commandments benefit us because they are geared at protecting us from ourselves and from others. Secondly, it is the manufacturer of a product that can give accurate information on how a product ought to be used in order to maximize its potential. In like manner, **only God our Creator can tell us what our ultimate purpose is.** This reinforces the fact that you cannot claim to be successful if you are not doing what God created you to do.

King Solomon recognized the emptiness that results in one's life if one does not surrender to God. It is important to look at Solomon's experience and subsequent warning for two reasons. Firstly, He had all the wealth and women that many crave after. Secondly, he had the knowledge and understanding that surpassed that of all the brilliant persons in the world. For Solomon to have come to this conclusion, suggested that he gave it a lot of wise and thorough analysis and reflection.

This suggests that it is worth observing his call, "Now all has been heard; here is the conclusion of the matter: Fear God and keep his commandments, for this is the whole duty of man. For God will bring every deed into judgment, including every hidden thing, whether it is good or evil" (Ecclesiastes 12:13, 14).

2. Bring All the Areas of Your Life Under The Lordship of Christ.

God must reign in every area of your life. "Commit to the Lord whatever you do, and your plans will succeed." (Proverbs 16:3). If God is being glorified in what you are doing, your plans will be established. Give everything to God and He will make it happen! Avoid the trap of committing to the Lord only what you think that you cannot handle. Ben Carson reminds us that we should never get too big for God (Carson 1992).

In bringing all the areas of your life under the Lordship of Christ, there are three important things you need to bear in mind. Firstly, your life and resources belong to Him. Secondly, you have been given stewardship over what belongs to God. Finally, you are ultimately accountable to God. These concepts suggest that God must reign in your personal life, professional life and public life.

Do not strive to do anything apart from God. Bring your finances, academic pursuits, career, business, dreams, aspirations, brain, time, treasure, talents, temple (your body) and testimonies under His Lordship. This is a recognition that you can only do all things through Christ who is strengthening you (Philippians 4:13). He must have pre-eminence in everything that you do so that He alone will get the ultimate glory. **Your pursuit of excellence must be through Divine Direction**.

3. Use Your Brain

Be a good steward of your brain. It is not unholy for you to use your brain; it is controlled by the Spirit of God when you surrender to His Lordship. You have engaged in unholy practices because you failed to use your brain. "…God has given to every one of us more than fourteen billion cells and connections in our brain. Now why would God give us such a complex organ system unless He expects us to use it?" (Carson 1992, 159). You used your cancerous brain instead and damaged your life.

"In his heart a man plans his course, but the Lord determines his steps" (Proverbs 16:9). The Lord directs the steps of the godly whenever he/she uses his/her brain which has been yielded to God (Romans 6:12-14). Stop complaining about what you do not have and start using what you have, your brain, which has been freed and liberated and emancipated from cancerous activities. If you are worrying about your plans, use your brain and allow God to direct your steps (lateral thinking). "Within the mind are all the resources for successful living" (Peale 2003, 51). Using your brain will also help you to understand that you can pray and ask God for direction.

It is important that you learn to think and allow God to control your life. This is so because if you allow others to think for you they will control you. Engage in brainstorming for problem solving and opportunity creation. Your brain is a gift from God that must be submitted to Him for transformation and used for the praise and glory of His Name. Romans 12:1, 2 clearly states "Therefore, I urge you, brothers, in view of God's mercy, to offer your bodies as living sacrifices, holy and pleasing to God — this is your spiritual act of worship. Do not conform any longer to the pattern of this world, but be transformed by the renewing of your mind. Then you will be able to test and approve what God's will is — his good, pleasing and perfect will."

Train yourself to think. You can do this by reading materials produced by critical thinkers. **Developing good reading and listening habits is crucial in learning to think critically and creatively**. When you read good material and listen to presentations with substance, it can spark creative and innovative ideas. "Reading is the way out of ignorance, and the road to achievement" (Carson 1992, 17). This is the concept of iron sharpens iron (Proverbs 27:17). That is to say, one person's ideas can sharpen another person's ideas. It is this concept that also drove me to get feedback from trusted colleagues and to read so many books in writing this book.

Seeing that you are depending on the use of language to develop your thinking skills, you need to work on improving your language. Develop a habit of using your dictionary and writing down principles, concepts and ideas. Sharpen your language skills so you can process material read and presentations listened to.

Here is an activity for reflection. *Imagine yourself in a big hall with several doors to get into several rooms. You noticed many persons waiting inside the hall trying to decide on which door to go through because they do not want to enter the wrong room. Some persons were either sleeping, behaving hostile, reading books, trying to interpret the plan for the building, having coffee and enjoying themselves or praying. Everyone must enter through the right door in order to maximize his or her potential. You noticed that some persons enter the hall and went straight through one of the doors. Some persons who were waiting in the hall followed them. What would you do to ensure that you maximize your potential? Put your response and rationale in the spaces provided below.*

....
....
....
....
....
....
....
....
....

4. Aim High!

It is correct practice that makes perfect. That is, if you are practising something and you are not trying to practise it the right way, you will not get better at it. It is worth noting that all the treasures of wisdom and knowledge are hid in Christ (Colossians 2:3). **The worst mistake is making the same mistake**. It is not ungodly to have aspirations. Aiming high will not cause you to move away from God because He is the One who directs your steps. Do not settle for mediocrity — honour the Lord in everything. Do well so that you can be promoted! Do well so that you can get the scholarships! Do well so that you will get onto the faculty that you want to get into! Do well so that you do not stay around and make life more difficult for yourself and your family. Do well so that your "relationships" will grow! Remember, you are an eagle; do not live like a chicken.

In aiming high, there are five important things that you need to remember. Firstly, believe in yourself. "Believe in yourself and release your inner power" (Peale 2003, 1). Secondly, connect with the right persons. Mark

Twain's warning is applicable, "Keep away from people who try to belittle your ambitions. Small people always do that, but the really great make you feel that you, too, can become great" (Motivational Quotes 2005 - Internet). Thirdly, learn how to prioritize and postpone gratification. "The Law of Sacrifice says you have to give up to go up" (Maxwell 1998, 84). Fourthly, do not compare your achievements with the achievements of others; set your own standard. Finally, move high in stages, rather than trying to be at the top in one mammoth jump. "A lot of us would like to move mountains, but few of us are willing to practise on small hills" (Motivational Quotes 2005 - Internet).

Have mentors in various areas of your life. These are persons who are outstanding. They should be persons you admire. This helps you to understand some of the things that you need to do to reach the top. These are persons whom you have decided to learn from, not to be their clone. Remember, according to Thomas Jefferson, "Nothing on earth can stop the man with the right mental attitude from achieving his goal; nothing on earth can help the man with the wrong mental attitude" (Motivational Quotes 2005).

> ***Here is an activity for reflection.*** *I learned a very important lesson from driving on bad roads. I discovered that when there were a few potholes on a good stretch of road, in order not to drive into the potholes I had to look at where I wanted the car wheel to go. If I focused on the pothole, I ended up in it. Therefore, I developed the philosophy that in order to achieve my goals, I had to focus on my goals. If I focus on the obstacles, I may miss my goals.*
>
> *I applied this philosophy or mental attitude when I did my Bachelor's and Master's degrees. As a result, no matter how difficult the assignments were, I was able to complete them and graduated with honours and high honours respectively. This was the direct result of focusing on my goals of high academic achievement, which gave me the enthusiasm, energy and generated urgency that I needed in order to forge ahead despite the challenges.*

How can this philosophy or mental attitude help you to aim high?

....
....
....

5. Seek Counselling

"Plans fail for lack of counsel, but with many advisers they succeed" (Proverbs 15:22). You need mentors or key persons in your life with which you can share your plans. I am saying, if you do not live in the right environment and feed on the right food, you are sure to die. "He who walks with the wise grows wise, but a companion of fools suffers harm" (Proverbs 13:20). Get various perspectives. It forces you to remain realistic. "The way of a fool is right in his own eyes but a wise man listens to advice" (Proverbs 12:5, KJV).

There is a belief in our society that when you seek counselling something is wrong with you. This is not a good perspective because persons seek counselling for various reasons. One of which is to prevent things from going wrong. Therefore, it is wise to seek counselling for guidance as well as to deal with personal problems and challenges. **Wise persons seek advice but fools allow themselves to suffer harm**. "You'll never know how close you are to a million-dollar idea unless you're willing to listen" (Maxwell and Dornan 1997, 82).

Sometimes brilliant ideas fail because persons failed to seek the perspectives of other persons or seek the perspectives of the wrong persons. There is a budding career field known as coaching. Professionals are now employing a coach to help them work through critical decisions to save them harm in the long-term. Even from this new career field, we are learning that it is prudent to bounce your ideas off some one who can ask you some critical questions about your decision.

Have you ever written something and read it over and over and thought it was correct only for some one to point out an error to you.

You were seeing what you thought you wrote through the writer's eyes and mind. This is why it is highly recommended that you get your academic and other important material proof-read. In like manner, sometimes in planning, you do not see your own pitfalls and possible precipices.

It is important for you to have various mentors. You need to have professionals in your life that are outstanding at various levels. You can have someone with whom you share your academic plans, another with whom you share your spiritual struggles and so on. It is also possible to find one person that can impact your life at various levels.

6. Divide and Conquer

"Go to the ant, you sluggard; consider its ways and be wise!" (Proverbs 6:6). The ant is strategic; she collects and stores her food little by little. No time is available for idleness. Keep working; do not look at how much you have to do; do it little by little and you will get it done. "Time is not an enemy unless you try to kill it" (Motivational Quotes 2005 - Internet). Be self-disciplined. "Do not love sleep or you will grow poor; stay awake and you will have food to spare" (Proverbs 20:13).

When you have a map of where you want to reach, you can move to the place in stages. You have to learn how to breakdown large goals or tasks into manageable pieces which will achieve the ultimate objective at the end. For example, if you have a book of five hundred pages to read and you know how long you want to take to complete it, you can divide the number of pages by the number of days that you have so that you do not pressure yourself unnecessarily. If you have ten days to read the book, the equation should look like this: $500/10 = 50$. This means that you would only need to read fifty pages per day to complete the book in ten days.

It has been said that the thief of time is procrastination. **Procrastination gives birth to laziness and idleness**. This kind of attitude causes you to waste time and pressure yourself in the long-term and do poorly. In dividing and conquering you value every minute. When someone asks you how many hours there are in a week, you are able to respond like if you were asked the days of the week. This is so because you know how you are going to spend every hour.

7. Believe in Yourself — Get Rid of Self-Destructive or Negative Thoughts

"Many are the plans in the mind of a man, but it is the purpose of the Lord that will be established" (Proverbs 19:21, KJV). This suggests that there are many plans in the mind which are good; the Lord will allow that which is according to His purpose to take place. Therefore, be careful of the thoughts that you have; think positively. **Do not impose self-limiting restrictions on yourself**. Get rid of cancerous activities in the mind. Mohandas Karamchand (Mahatma) Gandhi said,

> Man often becomes what he believes himself to be. If I keep on saying to myself that I cannot do a certain thing, it is possible that I may end by really becoming incapable of doing it. On the contrary, if I have the belief that I can do it, I shall surely acquire the capacity to do it even if I may not have it at the beginning. **(Motivational Quotes 2005 - Internet)**.

Know yourself. Identify your strengths and weaknesses, your likes and dislikes. Believe in yourself. You need to have a good understanding of who you are. Work through your struggles so that you do not allow things to cloud your God-given abilities. You need to develop a positive attitude. Tell yourself that you might not be good at it now but you have the ability to be the best. Remember; see yourself as a work in progress. **When you believe in yourself, you refuse to settle for mediocrity, which God does not want you to settle for**.

> Here is a concept for reflection. When I was growing up in Green Pond, South Manchester, Jamaica, we could not afford flashlight and there were only a few streetlights. In my early years, we did not have electricity. The toilet facilities and kitchen were outside, a little distance from the house. At nights whenever we wanted to do anything outside, a bottle torch was very useful.
>
> The bottle torch was made from a glass-bottle, into which kerosene was poured and then corked with a tightly wrapped piece of paper with a part of the paper extending above the opening of the bottle to form a wick. The wick was then turned down to allow the kerosene to soak into it. The wick was then lit. In order to keep the bottle torch going, the wick had to be soaked frequently by tilting the bottle to allow the kerosene to soak into the wick to keep it wet.

From this experience I learned that in order to keep negative thoughts out of my mind I had to keep wetting my mind with positive thoughts. In addition, in order to keep my mind functioning at the highest level, I had to keep wetting it by reading materials with substance. In order to overcome temptation and render the deceptions or lies of the devil powerless, I have to feed on the Word of God.

How do you think this bottle torch principle can help you deal with negative thoughts and help you to become a dedicated reader?

....
....
....
....
....
....
....
....
....
....
....

8. **Never Strive To Do Merely Your Best; Always Strive To Do More Than Your Best (Be Like A Good Athlete — Keep Setting New Records**).

If you ask Jamaican World Record 100 Metres Holder, Asafa Powell, "What is your next goal?" he would say "to do better than 9.77" (to be 'Afasa Powell'). "Brothers, I do not consider myself yet to have taken hold of it. But one thing I do: Forgetting what is behind and straining towards what is ahead" (Philippians 3:13). Keep building on your successes. Success should breed success. You must celebrate your small successes and move on. **You have the potential to be the best**. Don't "musturbate" yourself according to Albert Ellis (Corey 2000, 398) by telling yourself that things "must" work a particular way and become discouraged when they do not. Have the right attitude but not a "musturbatory" attitude. "Have faith in your abilities! Without a humble but reasonable confidence in your own powers you cannot be successful or happy. But with sound self-confidence you can succeed" (Peale 2003, 1). Remember that it is your God-confidence that gives you true self-confidence.

You must make a commitment to be better at what you do each day. This will cause you to move from the bottom to the top. Therefore, always strive to do everything to the best of your ability. Having discovered your weaknesses, you must dedicate time to work on your weaknesses. **Doing better must be your deliberate attempt each day**. You do not get better by osmosis. You get better by working hard at your weaknesses. Oliver Wendell Holmes said, "The mode by which the inevitable comes to pass is effort" (Motivational Quotes 2005 - Internet).

It is also important and practical to get a trusted friend or colleague to evaluate your performance. This gives you the kind of challenge and accountability that you need to grow and peak. This is also a very good practice to ensure that you are being a good steward of all that God has blessed you with. Myles Munroe (1996, 88) affirms this in his claim that, "potential is like soil. It must be worked and fed to produce fruit."

9. Speak Things Into Being

You should be familiar with the concept of "self-fulfilling prophecy." This asserts that what you say has a way of happening. That is, saying something either good or bad seems to give that thing generative power to happen. Therefore, you can tap into giving the things that you want to take place their generative power by speaking them into being. Speak it into being (the psychological concept of self-fulfilling prophecy is a good example of the power of speaking things into being), believe it, be expectant and avoid worrying.

Do not underestimate the power of the spoken word. Visualize what you want to achieve and when you have a mental picture of it, speak it into being. **Conceive it, see it, pray about it, and actualize it**. I cannot avoid being fascinated by the fact that we are created in the image and likeness of God and He spoke the World into being (Genesis 1-2). Therefore, with the image of God in us, we can speak things into being. Consider how powerful it can be when we are directed by God as Ezekiel was directed by Him to speak to the valley of dry bones (Ezekiel 37:1-10). That is to say, when we know what God wants, it gives power to our words.

Jesus Christ also spoke healing and deliverance into being. Seeing that we are called to become like Christ, we must follow His example and speak things into being. Activate your potential by giving it its generative power by speaking positively to yourself. **Remember that the spoken word has destructive and constructive power**. Your words either have poisonous or creative potential. Make use of this vital tool in maximizing your potential. **The spoken word has generative power when you are in line with God's purpose**.

However, there is a very important caution. There are times when you just speak things into being and watch them come through. However, there are other times when you need to speak and act. Look at how God created man in Genesis and how Jesus healed at times in the Gospels (first four books of the New Testament).

10. Learn to Deal With Changes

In order to achieve your goals and maximize your potential, you have to be tough-minded. This kind of tough-mindedness is not one that holds you captive to change but one that frees you to adjust to changes. It helps you to become creative and innovative. It causes you to refuse to accept defeat or setbacks.

In learning how to deal with change, you have to become a keen observer. Seek to know and understand the current trends. Make the necessary adjustments to ensure that you remain relevant. **Constantly assess your activity and see if it leads to productivity**. If your activity is not generating the kind of productivity that you are expecting, you need to do some revamping.

When you are aware of the trends you are better able to adjust to changes quickly. The antidote to dealing with changes effectively and efficiently is to be aware of the trends and be prepared ahead of time. This concept refers to the need to constantly sharpen your skills. Be a life long learner.

Deal with the things that are affecting your emotions negatively. This will help you to have enough energy to think creatively and innovatively to respond to change. In order to build your repertoire to ensure that you have a wealth of knowledge to draw from, be an avid or voracious reader. **Constantly cultivate your mind.** Practise emptying your mind of the things that siphon off your energy.

As you seek to deal with changes, remember that, if you want something that you currently do not have, you need to evaluate and do something differently to get it. **Don't be afraid to be a change maker**. Your dreams and aspirations put you on your "mark", your knowledge and skills get you "set", and your motivation keeps you going. Always remember that you are heading for the mountaintop and stay in the race. Be willing to make the necessary adjustments and move on. Allow your hope of winning to constantly give you the generative power that you need to win. **Learn to deal with obstacles by reaffirming that you can do all things through Christ**.

Reflections

1. Write a 1-5 Year Plan for your life.

   ....
   ....
   ....
   ....
   ....
   ....
   ....
   ....
   ....
   ....

2. Write a 5-10 Year Plan for your life.

   ....
   ....
   ....
   ....
   ....
   ....
   ....
   ....
   ....
   ....

3. Write a 10 Year and Beyond Plan for your life.

   ....
   ....
   ....
   ....
   ....
   ....
   ....

4. Make a list of the most challenging things that you have to deal with, inclusive of subjects in school or challenges on the job or in relationships.

   ....
   ....
   ....
   ....
   ....
   ....
   ....

5. Make a plan on how you are going to deal with each of them.

   ....
   ....
   ....
   ....
   ....
   ....
   ....

PART III

PART III

Facing the Future with Courage

In order to face the future with courage, have the right attitude. Therefore get rid of the bad attitudes that you have developed. This is important because the bad attitudes have caused you to develop poor habits. If you do not cultivate the right habits, you will destroy your life slowly.

Have a courageous attitude. Reflect on the past and live the present while making adjustments for the future. Your attitude will determine your aspirations, your aspirations will determine your actions and your actions will determine your altitude (how successful you become). Therefore, all that you will accomplish or fail to accomplish will be the direct result of your attitude which is affected or influenced by your thoughts and beliefs.

In this section, the focus is placed on your facing the future with courage. Chapter 8 will look at aspiring for excellence while Chapter 9 will help to develop coping strategies. In Chapter 10 the focus is placed on the fact that there are certain things that fuel low self-esteem that you can learn to deal with, so they do not work against you. In Chapter 11, the focus is placed on you yielding to God for your healing, restoration and wholeness.

CHAPTER 8

Aspiring for Excellence

In this section, the focus is placed on you facing the future with courage by aspiring for excellence. It focuses on three important principles, moving on, morality and motivation, to help you chase excellence against the odds. It seeks to reinforce the fact that you can succeed if you want to succeed. The Reflections aim at helping you to develop a strategic plan for your life as you seek to chart the path of excellence.

When you believe in yourself, you are able to chase excellence against the odds. Christian Nestell Bovee said, "Doubt whom you will, but never doubt yourself" (Motivational Quotes 2005 - Internet). The concept of chasing excellence against the odds clearly suggests four basic assumptions:

1. Excellence is achieved through a continuous process.
2. It requires effort in order to achieve excellence.
3. It is possible to achieve excellence.
4. There are things working against the achieving of excellence.

It also implies four important imperatives:
1. Do not settle for mediocrity despite the challenges.
2. Possess the power within you to become your best by God's grace.
3. Value excellence.
4. Choose excellence.

However, the main focus here is to help you to understand and appreciate your responsibility to chase excellence against the odds. We will seek to answer the question, "How do I chase excellence against the odds?" Here are three important principles, which will help you make it happen:

1. The Principle of Moving On

You are now on the verge of leaving the issues that have plagued your life. That is to say, you are now about to move on. This process of moving on is a part of life. This has to do with the fact that in life, there are changes that have to take place in order for us to be successful. Moving on from your past is one of those crucial changes that you have to deal with.

The bad news is that with changes come challenges. However, this bad news can become good news because you can change challenges into opportunities. You can change challenges into opportunities by developing critical thinking skills. The challenge is for you to learn how to think so that you will have power over your life and destiny.

You will have to make choices as you face changes and challenges. These choices that you make will have either negative or positive consequences. Therefore, be very careful in the choices that you make. You have no time to be careless and carefree. Make good choices to avoid conflicts, crises and chaos. Move on with a purpose to be a conqueror and not a sufferer. You must refuse to see yourself as a victim. View yourself as the victor. **Choose happiness and cultivate that habit**.

2. The Principle of Morality

As changes and challenges face you, it is important that you have some values that will guide the choices that you make. Have a keen sense of right and wrong. Be a person of impeccable character. Character is about who you are even when you think nobody is watching. It is about who you are as a person. Your character will cause you not to compromise the values by which you live for momentary gratification or striving to get even with those who have hurt you.

Be consistent in what you do. **Be willing to stand up for what you believe in, regardless of the consequences**. Ensure that your conduct is above board. Seek to conduct yourself in a manner that makes you, your family, teachers, friends and communities proud.

Become a good citizen, contributing positively to the development of your community and society. Take control over your own life and destiny. Take responsibility for the things that you get involved in and not get involved in things blindly because of past experiences that have kept you shackled.

Be careful with the company that you keep. Your friends or cronies should be people of integrity or good character. Keep away from crime and violence. Do not be afraid to make your concerns known in an attempt to deal with corruption and make life better for yourself and others. **Make a commitment to stay on what I call the HIT list, an acrostic for a person of Honesty, Integrity and Trustworthiness.**

3. The Principle of Motivation

There are two kinds of motivation both of which are important. You have external motivation and internal motivation. You can be motivated to do something by someone or because of your circumstances, which is external motivation or you are motivated to do something because you really want to do it, which is internal motivation. It is this principle of motivation that is going to help you to chase excellence against the odds.

When you are faced with changes, challenges, choices and conflicts, it is your motivation that is going to keep you going. When you are motivated you will be committed. Your commitment will help you to be courageous and develop effective coping strategies. You will be willing to collaborate with those who have the same vision that you have in your quest to contribute meaningfully to society.

Your internal motivation will cause you to postpone gratification for a higher good. There are things that you would want to do now but you will be willing to wait until the time is right. Your internal motivation will cause you to believe in yourself. You will have an internal conviction that you can accomplish your goals with God's help. Your motivation will cause you to seek to be competent at what you do. It will allow you to develop the confidence that you need. Remember "if you have no confidence in yourself you are twice defeated in the race of life. With confidence you have won even before you have started" (Garvey Memorial 2005 - Internet), according to Marcus Garvey. It may also be true to say that without confidence you are not even in the race of life. **Believe in yourself: God has given you the power within to be creative, innovative and constructive (practical).**

When you are motivated, you will be willing to compete in the race of life according to the rules. You will not be willing to live by chance, such as engaging in gambling and other things which are based on the principle of luck, but you will be willing to work hard for what you want. You will appreciate the fact that only grave diggers start at the top!

When you are committed to certain values, you will count the cost of excellence and be willing to pay it. You will learn to prioritize. You will never give up or give in but continue to work hard so you can give back. **It is your motivation, driven by commitment that is going to help you to move on successfully from the crossroads in life**. Prepare for the crossroads, so that when you get to them you know where to turn. Do not wait until you get to the crossroads before you decide which way to go. "The road to success is dotted with many tempting parking places. The one thing worse than a quitter is the person who is afraid to begin" (Motivational Quotes 2005 - Internet).

It is your motivation that is going to cause you to swim against the current while others are going down stream. You will be willing to stand up for what is unpopular because you know that it is right. You will not allow the current to discourage you because you are on a mission to fulfil your God-given purpose.

You therefore have the charge to make a commitment to be the best that you can be for the glory of God. Make the necessary plans for your life. What is it that you want to accomplish in the next 5 years, 5 to 10 years and 10 years and beyond? You must have a map of where you are going. Present them to God. Write your plans in pencil, so God can make His changes according to His will.

A Promise To Keep — Just For Me

Promise yourself to be the best that you can be in your career. Yes! Promise yourself to be at the top and not at the bottom. Promise yourself that you will not do anything because there is nothing else that you can do. Promise yourself not to stay at home and give your parents trouble and added economic pressure. Promise yourself not to become parents until you can pay rent. Promise yourself not to be a single parent. Promise yourself that your children will have both parents. Promise yourself that you will never get AIDS or other STIs because of a loose and immoral lifestyle.

Promise yourself that you will do well academically and get the scholarships. Promise yourself that your parents, teachers and friends will be proud of you. Promise yourself to engage in lifelong learning. Promise yourself to be different in a world of differences. Promise yourself not to complain about what you do not have but be willing to use what you have to get what you want (parable of the talents, Matthew 25:14). Promise yourself that the climax of your life will be of such that you can say, "Life was worth living." **Promise yourself to discover your strengths and weaknesses, and to use your strengths and work on your weaknesses**. Promise yourself to live by concepts that will enable you to live a fulfilling life. Promise yourself to be multi-skilled. Promise yourself to engage in wealth creation and in the process to take care of your health.

Promise yourself to discover and fulfill your purpose. God has created every one of us with a purpose. Discover and fulfill that purpose. Yes! You have the God-given power within you to become all that God wants you to become. **Never say you cannot: you can do it if you really want**. Pythagoras said, "No man is free that cannot command himself" (Motivational Quotes 2005 — Internet). Command your mind to think positively. You need to command happiness and peace.

Character — Commitment — Conviction

It is character that is going to get you out of bed in the mornings, commitment that is going to cause you to go on the job or to school and your conviction that is going to help you to deal with the changes and challenges. Make a commitment to go forward and maximize your potential and fulfill your purpose. Potential lies within you, like a rubber ball which must be properly stroked in order to bounce high; your potential must be properly activated. **Potential must be activated in order to be fulfilled**. Promise yourself to properly activate your potential and become bright, benevolent and brave.

Finally, chase excellence against the odds by applying the principle of moving on, the principle of morality and the principle of motivation.

The God-given power is within you! Go for it! Be a chaser of excellence; you can do it. Never give up; never give in; work hard so that you can give back. Remember, **there is one failure in life that you must accept, which is the failure to accept failure**. You will succeed not because you have not failed but because you failed to accept failure. Michael Jordan one of the NBA's greatest players said, "I have missed more than 9,000 shots in my career. I have lost almost 300 games. On 26 occasions I have been entrusted to take the game winning shot... and I missed. I have failed over and over and over again in my life. And that's precisely why I succeed" (Motivational Quotes 2005 - Internet).

Reflections

1. Having worked through your issues, make a list of the issues that you are moving on from.

   ....
   ....
   ....
   ....
   ....

2. Do you believe that some things are right while others are wrong? Why or why not?

   ....
   ....
   ....
   ....
   ....

3. What are you motivated to become and what kind(s) of motivation are you operating on?

   ....
   ....
   ....
   ....
   ....

4. Having decided on what you want to become, make a list of all the things that you need to do in order of priority, step by step to achieve your goal(s).

   ....
   ....
   ....
   ....
   ....
   ....
   ....
   ....
   ....
   ....
   ....

5. Make a list of the things that you are now promising yourself to be and do.

   ....
   ....
   ....
   ....
   ....
   ....
   ....
   ....

CHAPTER 9
Coping Strategies

In this section, the focus is placed on you facing the future with courage by focusing on your strengths and working on your weaknesses. It focuses on helping you to develop positive thoughts and reinforce them so that they become a part of your self-talk. It seeks to reinforce the fact that your thoughts affect how you feel and act. There is also an exploration of practical lifestyle issues that need to be regulated in order to cope effectively. The Reflections at the end of the chapter help you to discover positive thoughts and develop coping cards to help you monitor your self-talk. It always encourages you to take other practical steps to help you live a fulfilling life. It is worth noting that based on the importance of coping skills to deal with difficulties in life, someone has developed a whole theory on counselling known as coping skills therapy (Hansen, Rossberg and Cramer 1994, 153).

The concept in Ecclesiastes 3:1-8, that there is a season and a time for every matter under heaven, suggests that there are various issues that one has to deal with from the womb to the tomb. Sometimes you feel as if everything about you is screwed-up. However, there is hope.

It is important to develop strategies to cope with what Keith S. Dobson (2001, 339) calls automatic thought. The automatic thought has to do with your belief system. Therefore, when something happens you just react automatically without thinking. Thought is very powerful. It is important to develop strategies to help change your thought. Never take counsel from your cancerous or negative thoughts. **There is only one way to change your thought, which is learning to think differently.** In like manner, there is only one way to change your feeling and behaviour, learning to think differently. "The fact is, YOU FEEL THE WAY YOU THINK!" (Backus 1994, 15).

You can replace negative thoughts with positive thoughts by writing positive thoughts on index cards. These cards can be carried around with you and used when you recognize that you are thinking negatively. Used repeatedly, you will reinforce those positive thoughts and they will become a part of your automatic thought patterns. Your coping cards could contain the following:

1. "A simple man believes anything, but a prudent man gives thought to his steps." (Proverbs 14:15).
2. "A man of many companions may come to ruin, but there is a friend who sticks closer than a brother." (Proverbs 18:24).
3. "A gift opens the way for the giver and ushers him into the presence of the great." (Proverbs 18:16).
4. "He who gets wisdom loves his own soul; he who cherishes understanding prospers." (Proverbs 19:8).
5. "If you have no confidence in self you are twice defeated in the race of life. With confidence you have won even before you have started." (Garvey Memorial 2005 - Internet)
6. The most dangerous words are, "I can't."
7. "I can do all everything through him who gives me strength." (Philippians 4:13).
8. I am special because I am worth the life of God's only Son.
9. **I can Change Obstacles into Personal Empowerment (COPE)**.
10. I am a work in progress; God is working on me.
11. "Do not say, 'I'll pay you back for this wrong!' Wait for the Lord, and he will deliver you." (Proverbs 20:22).
12. It is not how you started but how you finished that matters.
13. I have the potential to become all that God has created me to become by His grace.
14. Marcus Garvey said, "…you must stop being what you are not." (Scripture and Race 2005 - Internet).
15. William Lyon Phelps said, "Real happiness is not dependent on external things. The pond is fed from within. The kind of happiness that stays with you is the happiness that springs from inward thoughts and emotions. You must cultivate your mind if you wish to achieve enduring happiness" (Motivational Quotes 2005 - Internet).
16. Carl Bard said, "Though no one can go back and make a brand new start, anyone can start from now and make a brand new ending." (Motivational Quotes 2005 - Internet).

17. Max DePree said, "We cannot become what we need to be by remaining what we are." (Motivational Quotes 2005 - Internet).
18. "Your true capacity is not limited, reduced, or altered by the opinion of others or your previous experience." (Munroe 1996, 8).
19. **I have rubber ball capacity to bounce high; I will not be a door mat**.
20. As the old adage says, "A candle burning at both ends finishes faster." I am not going to allow myself to burn out quickly. I have the capacity to put out the fire at one end of the candle.
21. Your mind is like a parachute; it must be opened to work properly and fulfil its purpose.
22. According to Eleanor Roosevelt, "No one can make us feel inferior without our permission." (Carson 1992, 179).
23. Believe in yourself and you will succeed.
24. **Like the caterpillar which possesses the innate capacity to go through a rigorous process and fly, I have the innate capacity to go through the process of life and maximize my potential, "fly"**.
25. "…begin to think prosperity, achievement, success." (Peale 2003, 169).
26. **If I see defeat I will create it, if I visualize success, I will create it**.
27. "If you're thinking defeat, change your thoughts at once. Get new and positive thoughts. That is primary and basic in overcoming difficulties and achieving.'" (Peale 2003, 173).
28. I shall achieve the best with God's help.
29. "Change the words you think and speak and you change the person you are." (Day 2003, 37).
30. **Stop! Visualize what you want, create it, believe it, pray about it and actualize it**.
31. "An inflow of new thoughts can remake you regardless of every difficulty you may now face…" (Peale 2003, 173).

It is important to develop positive thoughts because we are told in Proverbs 16:24 that "Pleasant words are like a honeycomb, sweetness to the soul and health to the body." Remember, words are powerful, used by us either to express ourselves to others or to express ourselves to ourselves. **Train your mind to be selectively permeable**. That is, learn how to block some things and allow others to pass through. Develop a strategy of choosing how you allow things to affect you.

The cancerous mind operates like a dry-rot sponge. Instead of absorbing the substance that it is working on, it allows the substance to run out. This produces more work and futile labour. This coping strategy can be seen as a part of the process of replacing the dry-rot sponge in the mind with a proper sponge. In psychological jargon, this is seen as restructuring cognitive errors which corrects what Aaron Beck (1976, 213) called blind spots, blurred perceptions and self-deception.

Develop strategies to deal with stress and tension. Music can be a good source for meditation, reflection, motivation and soothing. **Choose uplifting music that you can listen to whenever you feel down**. Choose your music carefully so that it reinforces your values. However, **be very careful of soul music and hardcore reggae. This is so because soul music stimulates sexual desires and hardcore reggae stimulates the pelvic area**. It is important to note this because music sets various kinds of moods. The good old fashioned waltz improves the condition of the heart and all western classical music uplifts the very soul. It has been documented by researchers that no one who loves listening to classical music ever touch drugs. Further, it has been researched and documented that a continuous exposure to this type of music raises the intelligence level, and provides a positive mind-set to excel in all endeavours. Outreach programmes based on classical music and good jazz introduced to inner-city problem children in the US have turned these children into model students achieving high grades in school to the amazement of their own parent(s), who repeatedly were unable to discipline them. This really is food for thought!

Develop a regular programme of aerobic exercise. Creative dancing could become a part of this. In addition, learning deep-breathing exercises to help you deal with anxiety is very critical. Nature walk and site-seeing can allow for reflection and time out. "There is one art of which man should be master — the art of reflection" (Motivational Quotes 2005 — Internet). Be creative and put your thoughts and motivational quotes in poems or songs. Finally, ensure that you get enough rest and eat properly. "Between each dawn and setting sun, set aside some time for fun"

(Motivational Quotes 2005 — Internet). However, you need to remember that too much fun now will deprive you of fun later. Strike the right balance!

You need to engage in what Norman Vincent Peale (2003) calls "mental catharsis" to empty the mind of negative thoughts. You can do this by spending about 15 to 20 minutes in silence each day. In order for you to stop your thoughts running, write down your troubling thoughts on a piece of paper. Burn or tear up the paper to symbolically indicate the death of those troubling thoughts. You may also pray and give God those troubling thoughts and other things that are running through your mind. Remember, they that wait on the Lord shall continue to be renewed in their minds. Bring yourself to total silence by picturing God in your presence or a pleasant scene or experience. After about 10 minutes, fill your mind with positive thoughts. Your coping cards can become handy at this point.

Reflections

1. Log on to the Internet and go to the http://www.innertalk.com/quotes.html and choose motivational quotations that you want to include on your coping cards.

2. From the suggested list of motivational quotes listed in this chapter, choose the ones that you want to include on your coping cards and record the numbers below.

....
....
....
....
....
....
....
....
....
....
....
....
....

3. Get some 3"x5" cards and prepare your coping cards.

4. Write a motivational song or poem that you can refer to when you feel discouraged.

....
....
....
....
....
....
....
....
....
....
....
....
....

5. Get a medical check-up to ensure that you can start your exercise programme.

CHAPTER 10

Things that Fuel Low Self-Esteem

In this section, the focus is placed on you facing the future with courage by understanding the things that fuel low self-esteem. It helps you to understand that when certain areas of your life are under control, it boosts your self-esteem. Special attention is given to improper goal setting, poor problem solving skills, poor decision making skills, inappropriate ways of dealing with anger and comparing self with others. The Reflections aim at helping you to develop life skills to boost your self-esteem.

There are various things that fuel low self-esteem. Some of these include:

1. Poor time management — "Love not sleep, lest you come to poverty; open your eyes, and you will have plenty of bread" (Proverbs 20:13).
2. Inadequate information
3. Improper association — "He who walks with wise men becomes wise, but the companion of fools will suffer harm" (Proverbs 13:20).
4. Dwelling or focusing on one's weaknesses
5. Failure to see self as a work in progress
6. Comparing self with others
7. Improper goal setting
8. Poor problem solving skills
9. Poor decision making skills
10. Inappropriate ways of dealing with anger

In this section, the focus will be placed on themes above that have not been dealt with in any way before in this book. The objective is to help you to understand that when you improve your life in some areas, it also improves your self-esteem. This has to do with the fact that success breeds success. Improving some areas of your life will help you to develop self-efficacy. According to Robert A. Baron and Donn Byrne (2000, 182), quoting Bandura (1977) "Self-efficacy is a person's evaluation of his or her ability or competency to perform a task, reach a goal, or overcome an obstacle…"

Improper Goal Setting

If you do not practise setting proper goals for your life, you will not develop a careful plan to achieve them, or you will be disappointed when you fail to achieve. This is the same as saying, "if you fail to plan, you plan to fail." **Failure affects one's self-esteem negatively, especially when one's self-esteem is battered and bruised**. Many persons have argued that our goals should be SMART, using smart as an **acronym for Specific, Measurable, Achievable, Realistic and Time-bound**. Your goal must be properly worked out. This will ensure that you set goals that are consistent with your skills, knowledge, experiences, competences and resources. Let us flesh-out the acronym SMART:

Specific

It is important to clearly state your goals. "Goals give us something to shoot for. They keep our efforts focused. They allow us to measure our success." (Levine and Crom 1993, 155). When goals are specific, it is easy to classify them as short-term, interim, or long-term goals. It helps you to make incremental steps towards your ultimate goal because you have the big picture in mind. **When your goals are not specific, it is easy to engage in meaningless activities**. Specific goals help you to develop a clear rationale or reason for whatever you do. A professor once said to me, "There is method in your madness" because I had a specific goal that I was working at achieving. Finally, specific goals allow you to take charge of your life. It prevents you from drifting around aimlessly by keeping you focused. It causes you not to follow the crowd but to follow your dreams.

Measurable

This is directly built on the specificity of your goals. You will only be able to measure your goals when they are specific. **Knowing what you**

want to achieve is the only basis on which you can measure your success. This concept of your goals being measurable answers the question, "How do you know that you are achieving the goals?" Therefore, the goals must be broken-down into small incremental steps towards achieving them. These incremental steps become the landmarks for measuring and evaluating progress. "Most challenges are best faced with a series of interim goal." (Levine and Crom 1993, 162). For example, if you want to become a good reader, how will you know if you are becoming a good reader? You can know this if you have a clear vision of what a good reader looks like. You can measure your success or progress based on your vision of a good reader.

Attainable

This is a crucial step in goal-setting because it answers the question of possibility and probability. It helps you to evaluate how possible it is for you to reach the goals. It evaluates your internal capacity and current level of functioning. It helps you to clearly classify your goals as short-term, interim, or long-term goals. It focuses on the things that you have direct control over.

Realistic

This works in tandem with the concept of attainable. However, its focus is external. It looks at variables over which you have no direct control. In setting goals, **you must ensure that you set them as realistic as possible to mitigate external forces that can abort your progress towards achieving your goals.** Your goals must be driven more by internal control than external control. A good way of ensuring this is to ask the question, will this goal make me more valuable in what I am doing and to the people around me?

Time-Bound

The concept of measurable only has meaning if you have a time-frame in which to work. It is not easy to measure your goal and say you are getting there if you do not have a specific time that you are working with. Levine and Crom (1993, 156), quoted Harvey Mackay who said, "A goal is a dream with a deadline." **There must be the necessary time limit to generate the enthusiasm, energy and urgency, which are critical for goal attainment.** This helps you to be disciplined and learn to prioritize.

Reflections

1. Using the acronym SMART, write out your physical, social, emotional, career and familial goals.

   Physical goal(s)

   ....
   ....
   ....
   ....
   ....
   ....
   ....
   ....
   ....
   ....

   Social goal(s)

   ....
   ....
   ....
   ....
   ....
   ....
   ....
   ....
   ....
   ....

Emotional goal(s)

....
....
....
....
....
....
....
....

Familial goal(s)

....
....
....
....
....
....
....
....

Career goal(s)

....
....
....
....
....
....
....
....

2. Review your goals and complete the table below, bearing in mind the question, what do I want to achieve during my lifetime? Or what do I want God to say to me on judgment day?

NEEDS (Things I do not want to do without)	**WANTS** (Things I would be happier with)	**PRIORITY** (Put your goals in descending order, starting with the most important)

Poor Problem Solving Skills

We all face challenges in life. Therefore, it is imperative that we all learn how to solve them without putting ourselves in deeper problems. You are required to do the following work activity before you continue to read.

Work Activity

Use four consecutive (without lifting the pen from the paper) straight lines to join the nine dots below.

• • •

• • •

• • •

This exercise has proven difficult for many. Do not be too hard on yourself if you were not able to do it. Let me explain how it can be done. The secret is to think outside the box. Start with the top row of dots, by drawing a line horizontally through them passing the last dot by about one inch. Draw an angle of a triangle from this point going through the third dot in the second row and the second dot in the third row all the way down stopping underneath the first dot in the third row. Draw a straight line from this point to the first dot in the first row. Draw a triangle shaped line from this point to the centre dot and the third dot in the third row. You should have now completed joining the nine dots without lifting your pen from the paper.

By now you should have grasped the point of this exercise. Sometimes your problem seems unsolvable but if you think outside of the box, you can solve the problem. It also demonstrates that sometimes you might have to seek help, by telling someone who has the competence where you want to go or what problem you are faced with, so you can get the help that you need to achieve your goal. You also might waste time at times trying to solve a problem that you need help to solve.

Don't be afraid to ask for help. Others had to be willing to ask for and seek help so they could be where they are today. The steps that will be dealt with in decision-making skills are useful in problem solving.

Poor Decision Making Skills

If you do not have a clearly thought out approach to make decisions you will have challenges that seem overbearing. You will end up making poor decisions and further crush your self-esteem. The following is a useful approach to help you make good decisions:

1. Clearly state the problem that you are having. **(Write it out)**
2. Brainstorm — look at various alternatives to solve the problem.
3. Look at the advantages and disadvantages of the alternatives by assessing the "possible results of alternative actions." (Ivey and Ivey 1999, 275).
4. Evaluate the ones with the best advantages using your values. If you are having challenges evaluating, seek help. Remember, "Plans fail for lack of counsel, but with many advisers they succeed." (Proverbs 15:22).
5. Choose the best alternative that is consistent with your values.
6. Act on your decision.

Work Activity

Choose a challenging situation that you are faced with and use the guidelines above to solve it.

....
....
....
....
....
....
....
....
....

Inappropriate Ways of Dealing with Anger

It is very important that one learns the dynamics of anger. Anger is a normal emotion. It is one of the protective emotions. It is not a bad emotion but if not handled properly can become destructive. Therefore, uncontrolled anger leads to aggression, which is destructive. Proverbs 14:17 declares that, "A man of quick temper acts foolishly but a man of discretion is patient." It is important to note that "no one but you is responsible for your anger…actions [done by others to you] may lead to your feelings, but you are responsible for your response" (Pelt 1997, 91). It is not correct to say that someone got you angry. You got angry because of what you thought about the person's action.

Your low self-esteem is fuelled by inappropriate anger management in the sense that it causes you to act inappropriately and then feel badly afterwards. It also causes you to hurt yourself or others in the process. Learn to control what you say and do when you get angry. Proverbs 15:1 states that, "A gentle answer turns away wrath, but a harsh word stirs up anger."

When you damage relationships with persons around you during your times of struggles, it is bad news for your self-esteem. It is during times of emotional and psychological struggles that you will need a lot of support. Therefore, you want to be careful about how you treat others so as not to cause further isolation. A friend sent me this email (author is unknown) which illustrates the destructiveness of anger very well. It is entitled "Nail in the Fence":

> *There once was a little boy who had a bad temper. His father gave him a bag of nails and told him that every time he lost his temper, he must hammer a nail into the back of the fence. The first day the boy had driven 37 nails into the fence. Over the next few weeks, as he learned to control his anger, the number of nails hammered daily gradually dwindled down. He discovered it was easier to hold his temper than to drive those nails into the fence.*
>
> *Finally, the day came when the boy didn't lose his temper at all. He told his father about it and the father suggested that he now pull out one nail for each day that he was able to hold his temper. The days passed and the young boy was finally able to tell his father that all the nails were gone. The father took his son by the hand and led him to the fence. He said, "You have done well, my son, but look at the*

holes in the fence. The fence will never be the same. When you say things in anger, they leave a scar just like this one. You can put a knife in a man and draw it out. It won't matter how many times you say I'm sorry, the wound is still there. A verbal wound is as bad as a physical one…

This illustration suggests that learning to control anger is critical. It is said that sorry can't make Harry. Proverbs 29:11 records that "A fool gives full vent to his anger, but a wise man keeps himself under control." **Learning to control your anger is always a win-win situation**. Proverbs 19:11 declares, "A man's wisdom gives him patience; it is glory to overlook an offence."

The first step in learning to control anger is an awareness of your triggers. That is, knowing the things that cause you to get angry. The second step in learning to control one's anger is the development of time out activity. These are activities you will do when someone triggers your anger. This is very important because "when you are upset emotionally, it is difficult to be rational or objective" (Pelt 1997, 90). The third step in learning to control your anger involves putting a system of reward and punishment in place for the control or lack of control of your anger.

Reflections

1. Make a list of the things that "trigger" your anger.

   ....
   ....
   ....
   ....
   ....
   ....
   ....
   ....
   ....
   ....

2. Make a list of the things that you will do when you get angry.

   ....
   ....
   ....
   ....
   ....
   ....
   ....
   ....
   ....
   ....

3. Make a list of how you will reward yourself when you control your anger.

   ....
   ....
   ....
   ....
   ....
   ....
   ....
   ....
   ....
   ....

4. Make a list of how you will punish yourself when you fail to control your anger.

   ....
   ....
   ....
   ....
   ....
   ....
   ....
   ....
   ....
   ....

Comparing Self with Others

There is a tendency for us to compare ourselves with others and feel badly about ourselves if we do not think we are like them. This is a faulty approach to life. **Every person has been given his special personality gift by God.** Your personality develops as you go through the stages of psychological development as you grow.

What is personality? Personality is the distinctive characteristics of a person that make him/her unique. It can be seen as the "traits that are fairly stable across situations" (Erickson 1998, 39). That is, you cannot assess a person's personality from just one particular situation. Personality is the characteristics that are ingrained in a person's way of being (feeling), doing (acting), knowing (thinking) and making decisions in the world (Kirwan 1984). The characteristics and traits of a person are seen as just aspects of his/her personality (Schmidt 1996, 217).

How do we assess a person's personality? The adjectives that you use to describe persons based on the way that they operate "give you a sense of the fundamental characteristics of each person" (Halgin and Whitbourne 1994, 141). There is nothing wrong with a person's personality as long as there is no "personality disorder, as well as prominent maladaptive personality features..." (Sue et al 1997, 88). This is supported by Carl Jung's study on human behaviour in which he "discovered that human beings have four essential preferences that shape the way they relate to the world around them and process the data they receive from that world" (Mulholland 1993, 51). Jung organized these preferences into four pairs, extraversion-introversion; sensing-intuition; thinking-feeling; judgment-perception. From these four pairs he found sixteen (16) basic preference patterns. However, even within these sixteen basic preference patterns there are a number of combinations. It is argued that preference pattern is like handedness, some use the right hand, some the left hand and some both hands. The use of one hand is not better than the other or the use of both (Mulholland 1993).

Your personality is your preferred way to be and act in the world. You are unique. **Nothing is wrong with you that you need to work through if you are well adjusted.** It is very important for you to process your hurt, pain and betrayal because both the conscious and unconscious minds operate in personal functioning (Crabb 1997), and a large part of our lives proceeds on the unconscious level. It is because of our uniqueness that all of us have to learn interpersonal skills, such as communication, conflict management, and impression management (for example, the clothes that we wear). It is also important for us to learn self-management and self-regulation skills.

> *Here is a case for reflection. When I was growing up in Green Pond, South Manchester, Jamaica, I was the last to get picked for a game of cricket or baseball. After both teams were through choosing whom they wanted on their teams, the team captains would agree for me to become "boaty", which means that I would play for both sides. I would only field for both teams, I would never get a chance to bat; even if I did, it had to be a desperate situation and I would be the last to bat. I felt left out and stupid.*
>
> *However, I developed a way of compensating for the weakness in playing cricket and baseball. I was good at climbing trees, making skater-bike, cartwheel, hand-cart and board-wheel cart. They had to look towards me for things to ride on. As a result of my skills in these areas, I was called "skill-guy." I felt proud to be called "skill guy" not "boaty".*
>
> *The weakness in not being able to play cricket and baseball became an asset. When my friends were out playing, I used the time to study and later to work on my serious challenge with mastering English. From this experience (and others!), I learned not to compare myself with others. I can allow my strengths as well as my weaknesses to work for me. Don't compare yourself with others; we all play important roles on the stage of life.*

Reflections

1. Describe your personality.

   ....
   ....
   ....
   ....
   ....
   ....
   ....
   ....
   ....
   ....

2. Do you find yourself wishing you were like someone else? Explain your answer.

   ....
   ....
   ....
   ....
   ....
   ....
   ....
   ....
   ....
   ....

3. In what ways will you stop comparing yourself with others?

....
....
....
....
....
....
....
....
....
....

4. What interpersonal skills do you need to develop to ensure that personality conflicts and differences do not weaken your self-esteem?

....
....
....
....
....
....
....
....
....
....

Chapter 11

Yielding to God

In this section, the focus is placed on you facing the future with courage by understanding the importance of yielding to God for your total healing and deliverance. This is so because healing is viewed as being wholistic. All dimensions of life are important but the spiritual dimension has far-reaching implications for all other dimensions. The basis on which you need to yield to God will be discussed; it is giving to Him what He has given to you so He can do with you what He created you for. He is able to give you the strength and the wisdom that you need to deal with your hurt, pain and betrayal in order for you to fulfil your purpose in life. The Reflections help you to yield to God for your wholistic breakthrough.

There is a false concept of healing that is being propagated by the secular materialistic and instant gratification culture. This concept of healing separates the spiritual dimension of life from healing. This is a false concept of healing because wholeness cannot be separated from the spiritual dimension of life. It is only by attending to the spiritual dimension of life that one can develop what Mark K. McMinn (1996, 45-52) calls an accurate sense of self, an accurate sense of need and an accurate understanding of healing relationship. Understanding self is important for healing to take place. In addition, accepting that we are not self-sufficient and by so doing admitting to our brokenness is also important for healing to take place.

Human brokenness and bondage have been brought about by the fallen state of the world due to original sin (sin of Adam and Eve) and personal sin. As a result of the bankruptcy of the false concept of healing and wholeness that is being propagated, "…human hearts are hungering for deeper realities in which their fragmented lives can find some measure of wholeness and integrity, deeper experiences with God through which their troubled lives can find meaning, value, purpose and identity" (Mulholland 1993, 11). This is possible only if we yield to God, the One whose plan and purpose shape our paths and direction for the fulfilment of our purpose, role and destiny.

Yielding to God enlivens and enriches your life. M. Robert Mulholland Jr. (1993, 16) emphasized,

> Rebellion against God's gracious work moves us into destructive and dehumanizing emptiness, into increasing dysfunctional lives that are self-destructive…only God can liberate us from our bondage, heal our brokenness, cleanse us from our uncleanness and bring Life out of our deadness."

It can also be said that He is the only one who can ultimately heal our hurt, pain and betrayal. God is the One who created you and has made provision for you to be re-created in Christ whose mission is to save the lost (John 3:16, 17), heal the broken-hearted, set the captives free, heal and declare God's favour upon you (Luke 4:18, 19). The healing that is available in Christ is multidimensional and multifaceted. "God cares about every area of our lives, and God wants us to ask for help" (Carson 1992, 253).

In yielding to God, you have to give up control of your life. The focus is not on what you can do, but on what God can do for you, with you and through you when you yield to Him. **It is only in God that you can find your true identity and individuality, your uniqueness, which clarifies your special mission in His creation**.

Yielding to God for your healing and wholeness is in your hands. He will not push. He stands at the door and knocks. M. Robert Mulholland Jr. (1993, 38), quoted George MacDonald who said, "He watches to see the door move from within." Accepting the confrontation through His word of your need to surrender and develop a personal relationship with Him, puts you on the way to wholeness. Yielding to God allows you to accept yourself, with what William T. Kirwan (1984, 85) calls your divided self composing of both a rejecting self (the feeling of shame, rejection and helplessness) and a needing self (the need for affiliation, affection and affirmation). This will allow you to become more loving, caring, patient, kind, compassionate, forgiving, humble, understanding, brave and assertive.

You yield to God because you recognize that He has given you that which you need to accomplish that for which He created you. Therefore, God is using that which He has given you to give you that which you need. A part of yielding to God requires that you start with what God has given you. Give your abilities, talents, gifts, hands, feet, mouth, ears, eyes, brain and tongue to Him (these are like vessels). God has equipped you with these resources to bring you what you need. Do not sit down and complain about what you do not have, start with what you have.

You might have some things in your vessels that God does not want you to have. Take them to Him and ask Him to empty the vessels and fill them with what He wants you to have. You can take your empty vessels to God by faith and He will fill them. You can also take your filled vessels of pride, anger, un-forgiveness, bitterness, hurt, pain, frustration, low self-esteem, poor performance and He will empty them and fill them with the right content.

It is impossible for you to accept yourself past your pain without recognizing that the spiritual dimension of life is important. In the face of a battered and bruised self-esteem, you can find true purpose and meaning in life by surrendering to the Lordship of Christ. This will cause you to do things out of love for God. The value system of a person, who surrenders to God, is of a standard that will cause him/her to want to be different in a world of differences. **It is in God that you will find the strength to deal with the hurt and pain that you have experienced**.

In a relationship with God, you do what you do because it is the right thing to do. It prevents you from operating based on feelings and what seems to be dominant in your culture. In this vein, social comparison, i.e., "our tendency to compare ourselves to others in order to determine whether our view of social reality is or is not correct" (Baron and Byrne 2000, 123), does not become the hallmark in determining what is right or wrong. Let us not forget that God's "laws and commandments benefit us and have a positive impact on our lives" (Myles Munroe 1996, 157).

It is God who created you and He is able to help you deal appropriately with the hurt and pain that you have experienced. When you do not see yourself as ultimately accountable to God, you do what you do because you are only concerned about pleasing yourself, which does not result in healing and wholeness. From the high relapse rate of persons trying to combat the tyranny of addictive lifestyle problems like alcoholism, drugs, promiscuity, which are the most difficult problems to overcome, suggests that persons need a power outside of themselves. Teen Challenge has reported a very high level of success in helping persons to combat serious lifestyle addictive behaviours. This is so because they lead persons to tap into the "Higher Power". God says, "Be ye holy as I am holy." Additionally, once you realize that your body is the temple of the living God, you will never abuse it with alcohol, drugs or permissive sex outside of marriage.

In light of the reality of the strength and capacity that one can derive from the Higher Power, Norman Vincent Peale (2003, 223), affirmed that "…there is no problem, difficulty, or defeat that you cannot solve or overcome by faith, positive thinking, and prayer to God." This suggests that in **taking God as a partner and developing the right mental attitude, you can deal successfully with any problem in life**.

Tapping into the Higher Power will cause the most significant change in your life, which will influence and spark other changes. You will be totally transformed. Take God as a partner on the road to recovery and on your journey to be successful in life. **You cannot get to the mountaintop (maximize your potential) by remaining in the valley**. Take God as a partner and you will get to the mountaintop, "For with God nothing will be impossible" (Luke 1:37).

Take God as a partner and experience His presence. Be constantly aware that He is with you. Develop a proper mental attitude in this regard. Seeing that He is with you, you can affirm "I do not believe in defeat. Continue to affirm that (aloud) until the idea dominates your subconscious attitude" (Peale 2003, 114). Finally, yielding to God will allow you to become shaped, sharpened and set to accomplish your purpose. Let me illustrate this:

> *In order for you to use a saw to cut a piece of board, it must be shaped like a saw. If you are going to get the job done, you need to ensure that the saw is sharp to cut the board. In ensuring that the board is properly cut, you need to ensure that the saw is set. I used to try using my father's dull and twisted saw to cut board when*

the saw that he keeps sharp and set was not available. I was never able to do a good job and maximize the use of my time. When I used the saw that was sharpened and set, I did not have to work very hard and the job was neatly done. However, whether or not I was using the good saw or the bad saw I knew that it was a saw because it was shaped like a saw. I could not set and sharpen the saw so I had to depend on my father to do it because it needed a special skill. My father asked me for the dull and twisted saw and sharpened it and from this point on I had no problem getting the jobs that I needed to do, properly completed.

You are like the saw. As a human being, no one can escape recognizing you as such because of your "shape". However, in order to fulfil your purpose properly, you must surrender to God so that He can sharpen and set you for your purpose, just as how I had to depend on my father to sharpen and set the saw because I could not. **You need to surrender to God to sharpen and set you to fulfil your purpose because you cannot do it for yourself**. St. Augustine's famous prayer is very applicable here, "Thou hast made us for thyself, and our hearts are restless until they find their rest in thee." (Benner 2003, 63). God is described as a Potter in the Bible, and he will continuously refine you in the fire, so that you come out gold, to His Glory.

May I allow it to be so, O Lord, May I allow it to be so!

It is time for my renewed beginning!
I am restored!
My regeneration, recreation, rebirth, renewal and retooling rescued me.
Yes! I am free!
My God-confidence has given me true self-confidence!

Reflections

1. List the filled vessels that you have that you want God to empty.

   ....
   ....
   ....
   ....
   ....
   ....
   ....
   ....
   ....
   ....

2. Write out a prayer to the Lord asking Him to empty and fill the vessels listed in Question 1.

   ....
   ....
   ....
   ....
   ....
   ....
   ....
   ....
   ....
   ....

3. Having worked through this book, describe how you felt about yourself before and how you are now feeling about yourself.

   ....
   ....
   ....
   ....
   ....
   ....
   ....
   ....
   ....
   ....

4. Write a narrative on what you want to accomplish in life, and what you want your life to look like at the end, and pray and make a commitment to God to make it happen. Remember, however, that you **must** seek that His will prevails.

   ....
   ....
   ....
   ....
   ....
   ....
   ....
   ....
   ....
   ....

REFERENCE

Backus, William. 1994. *Learning to Tell Myself the Truth: A 6-Week Guide to Freedom from Anger, Anxiety, Depression, and Perfectionism*. Minneapolis, Minnesota: Bethany House Publishers.

Baron, A. Robert, and Donn Byrne. 2000. *Social Psychology 9th ed*. Boston: Allyn and Bacon.

Balswick, Jack O., and Judith Balswick. 1999. *The Family: A Christian Perspective on the Contemporary Home, 2nd ed*. Grand Rapids, Michigan: Baker Books.

Beck, Aaron T. 1976. *Cognitive Therapy and Emotional Disorders*. Madison CT: International University Press.

Benner, David G. 2003. *Strategic Pastoral Counselling: A Short-Term Structured Model. 2nd ed*. Grand Rapids, Michigan: Baker Academic.

Bernard, Janine M., and Rodney K. Goodyear. 2004. *Fundamentals of Clinical Supervision. 3rd ed*. Boston: Pearson.

Carlson, Richard. 1997. *You Can Be Happy No Matter What: Five Principles for Keeping Life in Perspective*. Great Britain: Hodder & Stoughton.

Carson, Ben. 1992. *Think Big: Unleashing Your Potential For Excellence*. Grand Rapids, Michigan: Zondervan.

Chalfant, H. Paul. 1988. *Understanding People and Social Life: Introduction to Sociology*. New York: West Publishing Company.

Chapman, Gary. 2004. *The Five Love Languages: How to Express Heartfelt Commitment to Your Mate*. Chicago: Northfield Publishing.

Clarke, Edith. 1999. *My Mother Who Fathered Me: A Study of the Families in Three Selected Communities of Jamaica. 2nd ed*. Jamaica: The University Press of the West Indies.

Clinebell, Howard. 1984. *Basic Types of Pastoral Care and Counselling: Resources for the Ministry of Healing and Growth*, re. & enl. Nashville: Abingdon Press.

Collins, Gary R. 1988. *Christian Counselling: A Comprehensive Guide, Rev. Ed.* United States: W Publishing Group.

Corey, Gerald. 2000. *Theory and Practice of Group Counselling*. 5th ed. Australia: Brooks/Cole Thomson Learning.

Crabb, Larry. 1977. *Effective Biblical Counselling: A Model for Helping Caring Christians Become Capable Counsellors*. Grand Rapids, Michigan: Zondervan Publishing House.

Day, Alvin. 2003. *If Caterpillars Can Fly So Can I*. Lake Worth, Florida: Million Mountain Press.

Dick, Devon. 2002. *Rebellion to Riot: the Jamaican Church in Nation Building. Kingston, Jamaica*: Ian Randle Publishers.

Dobson, Keith S. 2001. *Handbook of Cognitive-Behavioural Therapies*. 2nd ed. New York: The Guildford Press.

Egan Gerard. 2002. *The Skilled Helper: A Problem-Management and Opportunity-Development Approach to Healing, 7th ed*. United States: Brooke/Cole, Thomson Learning.

Erickson, Marilyn T. 1998. *Behavior Disorders of Children and Adolescents: Assessment, Etiology, and Intervention*. Upper Saddle River, New Jersey: Prentice-Hall, Inc.

Garvey Memorial. 2005. http://www.marcusgarveylibrary.org.uk/memorial.htm

Gilbert, Kathleen R. 1998. *Marriage and Family 98/99. 24th ed*. Sluice Dock, Guilford, Connecticut: Dushkin/McGrawHill.

Gray, John. 2004. *Men Are From Mars - Women Are From Venus: The Classic Guide to Understanding the Opposite Sex*. New York: Harper Collins Publishers.

Halgin, Richard P., and Susan Krauss Whitbourne. 1994. *Abnormal Psychology: The Human Experience of Psychological Disorders, Updated with DSM-IV*. Chicago: Brown and Benchmark Publishers.

Hansen, James C., Robert H. Rossberg and Stanley H. Cramer. 1994. *Counselling Theory and Process. 5th ed*. Boston: Allyn and Bacon.

Harley, Willard F. 1997. *His Needs Her Needs: Building An Affair-Proof Marriage.* Crowborough: Monarch Publications.

Horton, Paul B. 1965. *Sociology and the Health Sciences.* New York: McGraw-Hill Book Company.

Ivey, Allen E., and Mary Bradford Ivey. 1999. *Intentional Interviewing and Counselling: Facilitating Client Development in a Multicultural Society, 4th ed.* Pacific Grove: Brooks/Cole Publishing Company.

Johnson, Spencer. 1998. *Who Moved My Cheese? An Amazing Way to Deal With Change in Your Work and in Your Life.* London: Vermilion.

Jones, Stanton, and Richard Butman. 1991. *Modern Psychotherapy: A Comprehensive Christian Approach.* Downers Grove, Illinois: Intervarsity Press.

Jordan, Pamela L., et al. 1999. *Becoming Parents: How to Strengthen Your Marriage as Your Family Grows.* San Francisco: Jossey-Bass.

Kirwan, William T. 1984. *Biblical Concepts for Christian Counselling: A Case for Integrating Psychology and Theology.* Grand Rapids, Michigan: Baker Book House.

Kollar, Charles Allen. 1997. *Solution-Focused Pastoral Counselling: An Effective Short-Term Approach for Getting People Back on Track.* Grand Rapids: Michigan: Zondervan.

Levine, Stuart R., and Michael A. Crom. 1993. *The Leader in You: How to Win Friends, Influence People and Succeed in a Changing World.* New York: Pocket Books.

Lutzer, Erwin. 1983. *Managing Your Emotions.* Wheaton: Publication Inc.

Mather, Cynthia L. 1994. *How Long Does It Hurt? A Guide to Recovering from Incest and Sexual Abuse for Teenagers, Their Friends, and Their Families.* San Francisco: Jossey Bass Publishers.

Maxwell, John C. 1998. *The 21 Irrefutable Laws of Leadership: Follow Them and People Will Follow You.*

Maxwell, John C. and Jim Dornan. 1997. *Becoming a Person of Influence.* Nashville: Thomas Nelson Publishers.

McMinn, Mark R. 1996. *Psychology, Theology, and Spirituality in Christian Counselling.* Wheaton, Illinois: Tyndale House Publishers, Inc.

Motivational Quotations. 2005. *Inner Talk: When Believing in Yourself Matters.* http://www.innertalk.com/quotes.html

Mulholland, M. Robert Jr. 1993. *Invitation to a Journey: A Road Map for Spiritual Formation*. Downers Grove, Illinois: Intervarsity Press.

Munroe, Myles. 1996. *Maximizing Your Potential: the Key to Dying Empty*. Nassau, Bahamas: Diplomat Press.

Narramore, Clyde M. 1860. *The Psychology of Counselling: Professional Techniques for Pastors, Teachers, Youth Leaders and All Who Engage in the Incomparable Art of Counselling*. Grand Rapids, Michigan: Zondervan Publishing House.

Nichols, Michael P., and Richard C. Schwartz. 2004. *Family Therapy: Concepts and Methods*. 6th ed. Boston: Pearson.

Nouwen, Henri. 1979. *The Wounded Healer*. New York: Doubleday.

Oliver, Gary J., et al. 1997. *Promoting Change Through Brief Therapy in Christian Counselling*. Eugene, Oregon: Wipf and Stock Publishers.

Peale, Norman Vincent. 2003. *The Power of Positive Thinking*. New York: Fireside, Simon & Schuster.

Peck, M. Scott. 1983. *People of the Lie: The Hope for Healing Human Evil*. New York: Simon & Schuster Inc.

Pelt, Nancy Van. 1997. *Heart to Heart: The Art of Communication*. United States: Editorial Safeliz.

Prendergast, William E. 1996. *Sexual Abuse of Children and Adolescents: A Preventive Guide for Parents, Teachers, and Counsellors*. New York: The Continuum Publishing Company.

Sacred Service. 2005. http://www.marcusgarveylibrary.org.uk/sacredservice.htm

Schmidt, John J. *Counselling in Schools: Essential Services and Comprehensive Programs*. 2nd ed. Boston: Allyn and Bacon.

Scripture and Race. 2005. http://www.marcusgarveylibrary.org.uk/scripture.htm

Simpson, Joanne M. 2002. *Why Heritage? A Guide to the Importance of Our Jamaican Story*. Kingston, Jamaica: Creative Links.

Snyder, Howard A. *Kingdom Lifestyle: Calling the Church to Live Under God's Reign*. USA: Marshall Pickering.

Stutzman, Jim, and Carolyn Schrock-Shenk Eds. 1995. *Mediation and Facilitation Training Manual.: Foundations and Skills for Constructive Conflict Transformation*, 3rd ed. United State: Mennonite Conciliation Service.

Sue, David, Derald Sue, and Stanley Sue. 1997. *Understanding Abnormal Behavior*. 5th ed. Boston: Houghton Mifflin Company.

Taylor, Richard S. 1989. *Principles of Pastoral Success*. Grand Rapids, Michigan: Francis Asbury Press.

Turner, Jeffrey S., and Donald B. Helms. 1995. *Lifespan Development*. 5th ed. Fort Worth: Harcourt Brace College Publishers.

Wachtel, Paul L., and Stanley B. Messer, Ed. 1998. *Theories of Psychotherapy: Origins and Evolution*. Washington, DC: American Psychological Association.

Warren, Rick. 2002. *The Purpose Driven Life: What on Earth Am I Here For?* Grand Rapids, Michigan: Zondervan.

ABOUT THE AUTHOR

David Samuel Green obtained a Diploma in Biblical Studies from the Jamaica Bible College, a Bachelor of Arts in Theology with a minor in Guidance and Counselling from the Jamaica Theological Seminary (Honours) and a Master of Arts in Counselling Psychology (High Honours) from the Caribbean Graduate School of Theology. Since 1997, he has been a pastor, youth director, guidance counsellor, counsellor, seminar and conference presenter and an inspirational speaker. He is currently the Pastor of the Pitfour Church of God in Jamaica, Montego Bay, Jamaica.

His outstanding achievements include being the graduate awarded with the highest academic attainment on his graduation day from Jamaica Bible College. He received the Practicum Award on his graduatin from the Caribbean Graduate School of Theology, for outstanding, dedicated Christian service and professionalism displayed in counselling practicum. He was recognized by the Ministry of Education, Youth and Culture, Guidance and Counselling Unit and the Jamaica Association of Guidance Counsellors in Education, for Exemplary Guidance Programme in Region One (Kingston and St. Andrew) for the academic year 2003-2004.

www.ingramcontent.com/pod-product-compliance
Lightning Source LLC
Chambersburg PA
CBHW020904090426
42736CB00008B/490